Life of the Party

A Family Comedy in Three Acts

by Marrijane Hayes
and
Joseph Hayes

A SAMUEL FRENCH ACTING EDITION

SAMUEL FRENCH

FOUNDED 1830

SAMUELFRENCH.COM

ISBN   978-0-573-61156-8   Printed in U.S.A.   #648

LIFE OF THE PARTY

STORY OF THE PLAY

The authors of those two outstanding hits, *And Came The Spring* and *Come Rain or Shine*, have now written another long play which is even more appealing and humorous than its predecessors. Here again is a lively, understanding study of modern youth and the modern family—warm and funny, brisk and tender and full of hilarious situations and dialogue. The Hughes family moves to Butterfield and begins to choose friends. They make mistakes, of course, but in the end they are wiser because of them: this is the theme around which all the fun is built. Mr. Hughes is to set up a branch office for his firm; flighty, funny Mrs. Hughes, being something of a snob at first, has high social ambitions. Oldest daughter Mildred, a college freshman, fancies herself in love with the snooty son of a bank president. Imagine what happens to their aspirations when studious daughter Jean, under the illusion that she is in love with smooth-talking Mike Tisdale (who arranges the party and dupes Jean into playing hostess), flings off her glasses and her reticences and becomes the life of the party. And what a party! Dapper Teddy, her brother, gets into a merry mix-up juggling four dates at once —until the girls get wise! And youngest daughter, Amy, a rowdy cheer-leader, falls in love for the first time. Neighbors object to the noise—to the extent of punching bewildered Mr. Hughes in the nose. The police arrive. . . . Jean is in for a hard awakening—and so are the others, including both her parents. They all become aware of the serious implications of what had seemed very funny; and what makes the play unusual and worthwhile is the wise readjustments of the characters to one another and to life. One of the funniest plays available to high schools.

3

MUSIC USE NOTE

Licensees are solely responsible for obtaining formal written permission from copyright owners to use copyrighted music in the performance of this play and are strongly cautioned to do so. If no such permission is obtained by the licensee, then the licensee must use only original music that the licensee owns and controls. Licensees are solely responsible and liable for all music clearances and shall indemnify the copyright owners of the play and their licensing agent, Samuel French, Inc., against any costs, expenses, losses and liabilities arising from the use of music by licensees.

IMPORTANT BILLING AND CREDIT REQUIREMENTS

All producers of *LIFE OF THE PARTY* *must* give credit to the Author of the Play in all programs distributed in connection with performances of the Play, and in all instances in which the title of the Play appears for the purposes of advertising, publicizing or otherwise exploiting the Play and/or a production. The name of the Author *must* appear on a separate line on which no other name appears, immediately following the title and *must* appear in size of type not less than fifty percent of the size of the title type.

LIFE OF THE PARTY

CAST OF CHARACTERS

7 males—10 females
(Extras if desired)

JEAN HUGHES
MILDRED HUGHES
AMY HUGHES
MRS. HARRIET HUGHES
MRS. VICTORIA COATES
SALLY FRAZIER
DOTTIE KIXMILLER
MARYROSALIE VOGULHUT
HOPE SHUTTLEWORTH
RUTH COATES

TEDDY HUGHES
TOMMY KING
MIKE TISDALE
MR. JESSE HUGHES
CHARLES COLLIER
WALTER LIPSCOMB
SNAZZY MITCHELL

ACTION AND SCENE

The scene throughout is the living-room of the Hughes' home in Butterfield.

ACT ONE: *Evening of a pleasant day in early spring.*

ACT TWO: *Eight o'clock the following Friday evening. (During Act Two, the Curtain is lowered for a minute to denote the passing of about three hours.)*

ACT THREE: *The following morning.*

LIFE OF THE PARTY

ACT ONE

SCENE: *The comfortable and tastefully appointed living room of the Hughes family.*

In the Left wall, downstage, is a door leading to the dining room and kitchen. Down of door is a straight chair facing room. Against this wall, up of door, is a bookcase. In the up Left corner is a stairway: two steps, a landing, and two or more steps leading off Left.

French windows are set in the rear wall; behind these is the terrace, with perhaps a few trees or shrubs in distance—exterior backing. (If convenient, it might help the action a bit if the terrace outside could be raised one step above floor level; if so, of course, a step leads up to French windows.) To the Left of windows is a radio; a hassock in front of radio. In the up Right corner is a desk, facing downstage, with a chair behind it; on the desk is a telephone.

In the Right wall an arch leads into the entrance hall; the outside slam door is out of sight. Door to closet up Left.

A comfortable lounge chair, facing the room, is down Right. A few feet to the Left of it there is another lounge chair, hereafter referred to as the Right Center chair. Down Left Center a large sofa faces the audience at an angle, and in back of this a long library table serves as a catch-all for the family's books, magazines, and general odds and ends.

Bowls of fruit or flowers, a candy dish, pillows,

7

pictures on the wall, photographs on the radio— these complete the furnishings. On the French windows are drapes harmonizing with the general color scheme.

TIME: *Evening of a pleasant day in early spring.*

AT RISE: MRS. HARRIET HUGHES *is seated behind the desk, telephone in hand. She is a chatty, pleasant little woman, given to sudden emotions, quick-passing angers, fleeting fancies and interests. She is extremely well dressed, a bit on the frilly side. Her voice and manner are flighty.*

MR. JESSE HUGHES *is the eternal father: a bit baffled, a trifle harassed. He is never bombastic, never pompous. He has a quiet wry humor. He smokes a pipe. At rise, he is looking over the paper, sitting on the sofa, legs crossed; as MRS. HUGHES talks, he occasionally raises an eyebrow or shakes his head, then returns to reading.*

MRS. HUGHES. *(Into phone)* Well, in Sheridan City —that's where we used to live, you know—I was a member of every club in town. Every *important* club, I mean—of course. And one day I said to Mrs. Koschnick, I said—well, no matter about that. You don't know her.—Oh, I do want you to meet my family. They'd love you. Just the four children, you know. And very well behaved, too, if I do say so myself— *(From upstairs comes a loud BANGING of fists on a door)* and talented, too.

AMY. *(From upstairs—wailing)* You've been in there two hours now. What are you taking, anyway—a bubble bath?

MRS. HUGHES. *(Into phone)* Leaders in school, too —before we moved to Butterfield.

TEDDY. *(From upstairs—muffled but loud)* Get away! G'wan—beat it. Holy Smoke, can't a fella even get ready for a date in peace?

MRS. HUGHES. *(Into phone)* You'll *love* them. *(Laughs artificially.)*

8

MR. HUGHES. *(Rises and crosses to stairs; calls up)* Hey—what's going on up there?

AMY. *(From above)* He's been in there literally hours, Daddy! *Hours!* And all my charm bracelets are in there.

MRS. HUGHES. *(Into phone)* We're really a very quiet family. *(Then simultaneously with MR. HUGHES' next line)* I'm sure we'll love living here—though it is strange at first.

MR. HUGHES. *(Calling upstairs—simultaneously with the last part of MRS. HUGHES' speech)* Teddy—what about it? Your mother's on the telephone.

TEDDY. Oh, all right! *(A DOOR bangs upstairs)* I'm finished.

AMY. And do you smell sweet! Wow!

(The DOOR bangs again. MR. HUGHES returns to the sofa shaking his head.)

MRS. HUGHES. And of course I'm a Daughter of the American Revolution. On my father's side— Really? Well, I'll telephone again soon. Goodbye. *(She places phone on desk, rises, crosses down to Right Center chair)* That was that nice Mrs. Coates. I don't think she really believes I'm a Daughter of the Revolution. *(Sits)* And what have you been doing all day, Jesse?

MR. HUGHES. Oh, I've been looking at buildings. And I think I've found one that will do very well—

MRS. HUGHES. *(Lost again in her own thoughts)* I can prove it. We had it all traced by a professional tracer—you know what they call them.—What were you saying, dear?

MR. HUGHES. I said the home office will be very pleased that I found a building for our branch office so soon after moving to Butterfield.

MRS. HUGHES. *(Again not listening)* You remember when we had it done. He said it looked very much like one of my father's ancestors was that little drummer boy—you know, the one in the picture. Or was it the one playing the piccolo? Well, anyway, it wasn't the one with the flag.

MR. HUGHES. *(Baffled)* Who wasn't?

MRS. HUGHES. This ancestor of mine—my great-great-great something-or-other. *(Rising — petulant)* —Jesse, haven't you heard a word I've said?

MR. HUGHES. *(Nonplussed)* No, I haven't. I thought you asked me what I'd been doing, so I—

MRS. HUGHES. You're very exasperating at times, Jesse.

MR. HUGHES. *(Subsiding—ironically)* I'll try to improve.

(He gives his paper a shake and resumes reading. MRS. HUGHES goes to desk and picks up a book—one of those best-seller novels in bright dust-jackets. During this, TEDDY'S voice, raised in song, floats not so melodiously down from upstairs and continues under following. JEAN HUGHES comes down the stairs. She is a high-school Junior, seventeen. At the moment her outstanding characteristics are: an extreme seriousness and lack of neatness. She wears unpressed slacks, very loose, and a shirt that might be either her father's or TEDDY'S, with the shirt-tails out. Her hair is tight to her head. She also wears glasses — very dark, horn-rimmed glasses. These manage to conceal, for the present anyway, her very real attractiveness and charm. She is reading a heavy book and munching an apple as she crosses to Right Center chair.)

JEAN. *(Talking through her apple)* There's too much confusion up there for anyone to study. Teddy's warbling and Amy's yowling. *(Sits)* This place sounds like a zoo.

MRS. HUGHES. *(Crossing to sit in Right chair)* I've been trying to read this book for months. It was so highly recommended by Mrs. Kunody at the last Literary Club meeting I went to in Sheridan City.

JEAN. *(Pointing upstairs)* Those two spend half their lives in front of mirrors. What does it get them?

MR. HUGHES. Dates.

JEAN. Who wants dates?

MRS. HUGHES. *(Pursues her own musings—as usual)* Frankly, I don't think Mrs. Kunody read it all the way through. It's not her type at all. The hero's a lamb, though. I wish there were men like him in real life.

JEAN. Daddy, I don't think I'm going to like this town. Maybe it's just me, of course. I don't mix very well. It's hard to make new friends, though. *(Bites into apple)* I don't see, really, why we had to move here at all.

MR. HUGHES. Because my company moved me—that's why. It's a big advancement, Jean.

MRS. HUGHES. He's a little like Rhett Butler—in the movie.

JEAN. Who is, Mother?

MRS. HUGHES. Frances Drake del Vayo, of course. He's part Spanish.

JEAN. Oh—that trash.

MRS. HUGHES. "Trash"? This book? Mrs. Kunody said—

JEAN. *(Rises)* I read part of it the other evening. It's a fairy story for adults. *(Crosses up to sit at chair behind desk.)*

MRS. HUGHES. Jean, you're getting pretty high and mighty lately for a junior in high school! *(Insulted)* Trash—a thick, heavy, inspiring book like this.

(TEDDY's singing has continued under all this. He shifts from one song to the other, thinks nothing of missing a note or two, rushes right on. Now AMY cries down the stairs—)

AMY. *(Upstairs—very loud)* Listen—!

(MRS. HUGHES jumps, JEAN lowers her book, MR. HUGHES half-rises. TEDDY's singing stops.)

MR. HUGHES. What?

AMY. *(Off)* Listen! *(Then before we see her:)*
Zizz-boom-rah—
Chaw-chaw-chaw—
Bulldogs, Bulldogs, Bulldogs!

(She enters now. Her face is contorted with a snarl to emphasize the cheer, her fists working excitedly. She comes down the stairs)
Mow 'em down, knock 'em down, go, go, go!!
(Crossing to Center, she assumes pose of cheer-leader and continues:)
Zizz-boom-rah—
Chaw-chaw-chaw—
Bulldogs, Bulldogs, Bulldogs—
Eat 'em up, chew 'em up, spit 'em out—
Bulldogs!
(Then a big one and she leaps into air, leading an imaginary grandstand in the cheer)
BUTTERFIELD BULLDOGS! H'RAY!!
(Breathless, she pauses, looks at the OTHERS, *awaiting their approval.* AMY *is a Sophomore; she is lively, quick, and has promise of fair beauty in time to come. Her face is mobile and alive; her impulses quick and her usual gait a half-run. She wears sweater and skirt, low-heeled saddle shoes and bobby sox. Clanking bracelets cover her arm up to her elbow)*
Well, what do you think?

JEAN. Pass the aspirin, Moron.

MR. HUGHES. What is it?

AMY. *(Enthusiastically)* It's my new cheer. I'm going to revise the whole cheering set-up in Butterfield. It's creaky. I'm making up a whole new set of cheers. This is the first one. Isn't it yummy?

MR. HUGHES. Very yummy. "Eat 'em up, chew 'em up, spit 'em out"—um-hum, *very* yummy.

AMY. *(Starting for hall Right)* It'll curdle 'em.

MR. HUGHES. Hey, hold on a minute, Amy. Have you finished your homework?

AMY. *(Stops)* Homework? Oh, that stuffy dribble. Sure—hours ago.

MR. HUGHES. All of it?

AMY. Sure—I mean—well—

MR. HUGHES. I thought not. I think you'd better finish it. *(Appeals to* MRS. HUGHES) Don't you, Harriet?

AMY. *(Returning to Center)* Daddy—the "Slicks"

are meeting in five minutes. I've got to be there. I'm a new member and—

MR. HUGHES. Amy, what in the name of heaven are the "Slicks"?

AMY. The sub-deb club I belong to now. It's a lot smoother than the one in Sheridan City. "Slicks" means —"So Long, I Can't Kiss." The first letters, see. "S-L-I-C-K."

MR. HUGHES. (Lost—to MRS. HUGHES) Harriet, do you think she ought to go out before—

MRS. HUGHES. Oh, don't be that way, Jesse. They're only young once. (To AMY) —And Amy, if Mrs. Coates' daughter should be there, you be sure to tell her —well, don't *tell* her—but kind of *hint*, you know, that I expect to be invited into the Clover Club.

AMY. *(Crosses to* MRS. HUGHES) Mother, I can't do a thing like that. I don't want to get labelled icky.

MRS. HUGHES. Now Amy—just remember what I said. And you might mention that you're going to be a little Daughter of the American Revolution yourself some day. That'll impress them.

AMY. Yeah, that'll impress 'em. If I said a thing like that, they'd *kill* me at initiation. Well, so-long, Jackson. *(Exits Right.)*

MR. HUGHES. *(Under his breath)* "So Long, I Can't Kiss." *(Shakes head.)*

MRS. HUGHES. What did you say, dear? *(Then rushing right on)* Amy probably doesn't realize what an honor it would be for me to be invited into the Clover Club. After all, it's been in existence since 1879 and—

(TEDDY'S *song has grown louder as he has come closer to the stairs and now he is descending.* TEDDY HUGHES *is a Senior. He is "dressed to kill"— sports coat, brown and white shoes, bright sports shirt; every crease in sharp place. What he lacks in good looks he makes up for in his attitude: at once sophisticated and naive. He always attempts a suave, man-of-the-world pose, but sometimes fails.* TEDDY *stops on the landing, finishes the song with a little trill and a half-bow generally, mocking but pleased with himself.)*

JEAN. *(Squeals like a girl who has just heard Frank Sinatra sing. Then flatly:)* What are we supposed to do now—throw flowers?

TEDDY. You can't expect your own family to appreciate you. *(Crosses toward Right.)*

MRS. HUGHES. You look pretty, Ted.

TEDDY. "Pretty!" Mother, you swamp me. Anything but "pretty"!

MRS. HUGHES. Isn't that a nice word any more, Teddy? In my day—

MR. HUGHES. I suppose you've finished your lessons, Ted?

TEDDY. *(With a gesture)* Finished 'em? With one hand and half a brain.

(MRS. HUGHES reads again.)

JEAN. What else could you finish them with?

(TEDDY flashes her a dirty look.)

MR. HUGHES. In the bathroom, I suppose—while you combed your hair.

TEDDY. Let Jean do the studying for this family. She's a dull tone anyway.

JEAN. *(Angry, half-rising)* Listen, I—

MR. HUGHES. *(Quickly)* That's enough.

MRS. HUGHES. *(Looking up from the book—to* MR. HUGHES) Jesse, why do you want to be that way? They're only young once.

MR. HUGHES. I know. But they can't spend half their lives in high school. I can't afford it.

TEDDY. Did I ever flunk? Just once, did I ever flunk, I ask you— *(In a smaller voice)* besides history?

MR. HUGHES. *(Matter-of-fact)* English 7B.

TEDDY. That doesn't count. Miss Brown had it in for me.

MR. HUGHES. *(Rising)* The point is, Ted, that—

MRS. HUGHES. Oh, go on and have a good time, Teddy. Do you have a date?

MR. HUGHES. Now please listen to me a min—

TEDDY. *(Crossing to* MRS. HUGHES*)* With the smoothest little operator you ever saw.

MR. HUGHES. *(Giving up, sits again)* All right. But don't expect me at your graduation.

TEDDY. Why not?

MR. HUGHES. I'll be too old. If your grey hair won't embarrass you, my crutches might.

TEDDY. You know, I might bring this gal here to meet you later. It kind of impresses a girl to let her meet your family. She knows you're a straight Joe then.

JEAN. You're going to hang yourself with that line some day, little brother.

TEDDY. *(Crossing to* JEAN*)* "Little"? I'm older than you—fourteen months. You ought to whip up a line yourself, Jean. Remember: a good line is the shortest distance between two dates.

JEAN. No, thanks— By the way, little boy, what will Sally Frazier think about all these dates?

TEDDY. Sally Frazier is safe in Sheridan City. Besides, we're not a gruesome twosome.

JEAN. I hope she's double-crossing you the way you're double-crossing her.

TEDDY. *(With a wave of the hand)* Not a chance. Not good ole Sally— *(Starts blithely for Right door, pauses, turns to* JEAN*)* Saaay— *(*JEAN *pretends not to have heard.* TEDDY *leans across desk)* You mean you think Sally's stepping out of halter back there in Sheridan City?

JEAN. Sally's not the type to sit home with a good book—if you know what I mean.

TEDDY. *(Angered)*. Say—she can't do that to me! The little two-timer! I'm gonna write her a letter.

(The DOORBELL rings. MR. HUGHES *~ises and crosses into hall.)*

TEDDY. I think I'll write her a letter tonight! *(Starts to stairs. Pauses)* No, not tonight. I got a date tonight.

(Musing) Golly, I never thought Sally Frazier would do a thing like that. *(Remains behind sofa.)*

MRS. HUGHES. Jean, put that apple away. You don't know who it might be.

JEAN. Whoever it is, Mother, they've seen an apple before.

(MR. HUGHES *returns with* OFFICER WALTER LIPSCOMB. LIPSCOMB *is a tough and gravel-voiced cop who has spent most of his life on the police force. As a consequence, he is not very well mannered but very conscious of his authority. He is easily aroused and even more easily confused.)*

LIPSCOMB. Does that rattletrap of a car out there belong to you, Mr.—uh—uh—

MR. HUGHES. *(Near Right door)* Hughes.

LIPSCOMB. *(Looking him over)* New here, ain't you?

MR. HUGHES. Yes, Officer, we are.

LIPSCOMB. Well, you might as well get acquainted with our laws right away. *(Fists on hips; lecturing:)* In Butterfield there is a specific city ordinance against parking cars in front of fire hydrants. *(With heavy irony)* Does that sound strange to you?

MR. HUGHES. Look here, Officer—I see no reason for you to take that tone of voice. If there's anything—

LIPSCOMB. Listen, Bud—this is my beat, see. A nice, quiet, friendly neighborhood, you might say. I drive round and round all day—never any trouble. You got that?

MR. HUGHES. Well, we're sorry that—

LIPSCOMB. *(Glaring anyway)* What would a full-grown man like you want with a car like that anyway? No top, painted yellow and red, at least four horns on it, and no hood. And all those girls' names.

MR. HUGHES. *(Flustered)* But that's not my— I didn't say—

LIPSCOMB. *(Final judgment)* It's kind of silly, I think.

MR. HUGHES. *(Turning on TEDDY)* Ted—

TEDDY. Don't look at me. You know it's not *my* car.

(Desperately) Not—my—car—because I *(Bursting into song)* I haven't got a driver's license, ta-ta-ta-ta-taaa!

LIPSCOMB. *(Eyeing* TEDDY *with a great deal of suspicion)* Say—what's the matter with this squirt?

TEDDY. Who—me? I'm a singer. Practice all the time. *(Takes a stance and lets out with a very loud, blasting song. Then smiles ingratiatingly)* See?

LIPSCOMB. *(Frowning—turns to* MR. HUGHES*)* Let's see your driver's license.

*(*TEDDY *starts for stairs.)*

MR. HUGHES. *(To* TEDDY*)* Teddy, where's—

*(*TEDDY *turns on stairs—he starts making all kinds of idiotic motions to tell his father that he has no license.)*

MRS. HUGHES. Officer— *(*LIPSCOMB *turns to her)* —doesn't it get awfully tiresome riding around all day like that? I've often wondered. Don't you get—well, tired?

LIPSCOMB. Lady, I get tired, blistered and bored— but it's a job. *(Turns to find* TEDDY *signalling and making faces at his father)* —Say, I don't mean no disrespect or anything, but is that boy all right? I mean—is he normal?

MR. HUGHES. Officer, I've had about enough of this. You have no right to come into my house and call my family abnormal. *(Draws billfold from pocket)* Here's my license. Give me a ticket if you wish, but do it fast and get out of here.

LIPSCOMB. *(Really tough now)* Listen, Bud—

MR. HUGHES. And stop calling me "Bud"!

LIPSCOMB. *(Drawing himself up)* Listen, *Bud*—nobody tells me to get out of any place! I don't like the looks of this whole set-up one little bit, and—

JEAN. Say, I'm trying to study.

LIPSCOMB. *(Scowling at* JEAN*)* One little bit, see! *(Crossing in front of* MR. HUGHES *toward* TEDDY *and* *indicating* TEDDY *with a jerk of the thumb)* That kid acts batty. *(Then to* JEAN*)* And looking the way you do, you could be anybody or anything! *(To* MR. HUGHES*)* And I'm gonna overlook your impertinence to an officer of the law—*this* time—and I ain't even gonna give you a ticket—*this time*—but—

(At this unhappy moment MILDRED HUGHES, *a college freshman, enters from hall Right. The front door slams behind her.* MILDRED *wears a "Freshie" cap and looks a bit bedraggled—but nothing can hide the fact that she is an attractive, pleasant girl. She carries several books.)*

MILDRED. Daddy—what is it? Why are the police here? *(Crosses to him)* What have you done now?

MR. HUGHES. *(Taken aback)* "—Done now"? Mildred, what are you—

LIPSCOMB. *(Stepping right in)* "What have you done now?" Just like I thought. Say, you been mixed up with the police before?

MR. HUGHES. Of course not. I don't—

LIPSCOMB. This your daughter? Well, why would a girl say a thing like that to her father? That's what I want to know.

MR. HUGHES. *(Baffled)* I don't know myself. It doesn't make sense.

LIPSCOMB. You ever been mixed up with the police before? Ever been arrested?

MR. HUGHES. Well—yes—once—

LIPSCOMB. Now we're getting somewheres—

MR. HUGHES. But that was in 1917. I was in the Army then. I—

LIPSCOMB. What'd you do?

MR. HUGHES. *(Confused)* I socked a cop.

LIPSCOMB. Why?

MR. HUGHES. Well, because—

LIPSCOMB. He was trying to arrest you and you socked him—is that right?

MR. HUGHES. *(Crosses to sink weakly to sofa— swallowing)* No. I—

ACT I

LIPSCOMB. *(Following)* Come on—stop stalling.

JEAN. Dad—he can't do this! Legally, he's over his head. You don't have to answer.

MRS. HUGHES. Why, Jesse, I didn't know you were ever arrested. Just think—all these years—

MR. HUGHES. *(Appealing)* Harriet—Mildred—Jean —Teddy—for heaven's sake—I didn't do anything. He was a French cop. He was trying to take my girl away from me.

LIPSCOMB. Huh! You expect me to believe that?

MRS. HUGHES. Why, Jesse—do you mean a *French* girl?

MR. HUGHES. *Oui*—I mean: sure. A French girl—it was in Paris. What kind of girls do you think they have in Paris—Eskimoes?

LIPSCOMB. All right, all right—I don't want to get mixed up in any family stuff. *(Starts toward hall)* But just remember, all of you—I'm going to keep my eye on this house!

(LIPSCOMB *goes into hall and the front DOOR slams. There is a long pause. Then* TEDDY *recovers first; goes to* MR. HUGHES *around Left arm of sofa.)*

TEDDY. So you batted a French cop, eh, Pop? I didn't know you had it in you.

MR. HUGHES. *(Rising)* Where's your driver's license?

TEDDY. Oh—well, you see, I—I just kind of lost it and then I was kind of broke and I couldn't get another one, so—

MR. HUGHES. So you can just kind of not drive until you get one. Starting tonight.

TEDDY. Not tonight. Start tomorrow, Dad—cause I got a heavy schedule tonight. *Very* heavy.

MRS. HUGHES. You be careful and don't have any accident, then, Teddy.

TEDDY. *(Starting for hall)* Thanks, Mother—you're a dreamboat.

MR. HUGHES. *(Raising his voice)* Just a minute! I said—

MRS. HUGHES. *(To* MR. HUGHES*)* Was she pretty, Jesse?

MR. HUGHES. *(Thrown for a loss)* What? Who?

MRS. HUGHES. That French girl. She must have been awfully pretty if you fought over her.

(TEDDY disappears; the door doesn't slam.)

MR. HUGHES. It was a matter of pride. For Pete's sake, Harriet—that was a long time before we were married. *(Turning to where* TEDDY *stood and stepping to Center)* —Now, Teddy, I—

MILDRED. *(Crosses to flop on sofa—the picture of weariness)* He's gone. Whew, what a day! What a night! What was all the excitement about anyway?

MR. HUGHES. *(Turning on* MILDRED*)* Mildred, what would make you come dashing in here and ask a question like you did? As though I were some kind of a hardened criminal!

MILDRED. Don't pick on me, Daddy. I'm tired.

MR. HUGHES. It's a wonder he didn't take me in. *(Sits in Right Center chair.)*

JEAN. Don't pick on Mildred. Mildred's in love.

MILDRED. Maybe I am, maybe I'm not. Jealous, Jean?

JEAN. Of some dumb college boy? Who hasn't even called you up? Don't be silly.

MILDRED. He's not a dumb college boy. He's Charles Collier, if you want to know. His father practically owns a bank, dear—and his mother's *the* social bug of the whole town.

MRS. HUGHES. She is? And the boy's interested in you, Mildred? Isn't that nice? Jesse, did you hear that?

MR. HUGHES. I heard it.—Why is it that, every time I try to talk seriously to one of my children, either you tell them to do the opposite of what I tell them or we get involved in a discussion of puppy love?

MILDRED. *(Insulted)* I'm glad you think it's puppy love, Daddy. Maybe you just don't know.

MR. HUGHES. Mildred, I don't know anything. I came to that conclusion ten minutes ago. If his father owns a bank, that's enough for your mother. What do you want for a wedding present?

MILDRED. *(Wailing)* Daddy, we haven't even had a date yet.

MR. HUGHES. Be sure to tell him your old man's a jailbird.

MILDRED. You just don't care about anything. Do you know what I've been doing ever since three o'clock this afternoon? Scrubbing floors—on my hands and knees—and washing windows, literally millions of them! *(She is working herself up now)* Just because I'm a pledge!

MR. HUGHES. Do you mean to tell me I'm paying three hundred dollars a year so that you can scrub floors for that sorority?

MILDRED. Daddy, you don't understand anything! Not anything! *(She is beginning to weep)* No wonder I said what I did when I came in. Everyone's always picking on me!

*(Crying very loud, she stomps up the stairs and off.
MR. HUGHES braces himself and, sure enough, a
DOOR slams upstairs.)*

MR. HUGHES. Well, there goes Mildred.

MRS. HUGHES. Jesse, what's come over you all of a sudden? You didn't used to be like this. You liked to see your children have some enjoyment. *(Crossing to stairs)* Getting involved with policemen, hitting gendarmes in the face, and having dates with French girls. *(Shaking head, disappears.)*

*(A moment's silence. MR. HUGHES doesn't move. JEAN,
smiling, rises and comes down to sit on sofa.)*

JEAN. *(Lightly)* Daddy, you're a villain.

MR. HUGHES. I'm beginning to think so.

JEAN. I know what you're trying to do—I understand.

MR. HUGHES. *(Reasonably trying to figure it out)* I

don't object to fun. I *like* fun. I want you kids to have fun.—What's the matter with everyone all of a sudden?

JEAN. A lot. *(Rises. Crosses Left.)*

MR. HUGHES. *(Looking after her)* Yes, I'm beginning to think so.—You're the only one who doesn't have to study and—

JEAN. *(Softly)* And it's all I do. I know.

MR. HUGHES. No, I didn't mean that.—But why don't you go out and have a good time occasionally, Jean?

JEAN. *(Turned away from him)* You have to be asked, Daddy.

MR. HUGHES. Well, sure. I mean: I know that. But maybe if you'd—I don't know—fix your hair a little— get some different glasses— *(Pauses)* Well, thank God you've got some sense anyway.

JEAN. *(Turns on him)* I don't want to have sense. What do you think of that? I hate brains—especially *my* brains. They're the worst brains in the world. I want to like boys my age, I want to be in love, even— what do you think of that? I don't want to think boys are ridiculous—even though they always *act* ridiculous. I'd rather be like Mildred or Teddy—or even Amy— than the way I am—just a—a—a dull tone!

(She also dashes up the stairs. MR. HUGHES braces himself again, closes his eyes, waits. A long pause. No door slams. He half-smiles, satisfied. Just as he relaxes, the DOOR upstairs slams — hard! MR. HUGHES walks up to French windows, opens them, stands looking out. He looks down.)

MR. HUGHES. *(To himself)* Too bad this isn't a penthouse. *(He turns to the desk, picks up the book JEAN has left lying there; reads title aloud)* "A Psychological Study of the Modern Parent."

(He thinks it over briefly, then drops the book like a hot cake onto the desk, dusts off his hands, takes a deep and baffled breath, steps away. But his inter-

est is caught: he returns to the desk, picks up book, looks around sheepishly and crosses down to Right Center chair, sits, opens book. Just as he gets settled, the DOORBELL rings. MR. HUGHES *groans, rises, crosses to hall. In a moment he returns with* MIKE TISDALE. MIKE *is a Senior, a tall boy, carelessly dressed, not quite handsome but overwhelming: a smooth talker, charming, convincing, perhaps a trifle too loud now and then. Especially now.)*

MIKE. So you're little Jean's father. What do you know! *(Without being asked, he sits in Right Center chair.)*

MR. HUGHES. *(Crossing to Center)* Let me get this straight. You've come to see Jean, is that right?

MIKE. Yeah—Jean. Sure.

MR. HUGHES. *(Not quite believing it yet)* Jean Hughes?

MIKE. If that's all right with you. Great little girl—Jean. Smart, too. *(Rises. He presses his hand in the seat of the chair, shakes head. Then crosses to sofa, tests it for softness, smiles, sits. Then explaining:)* Softer. *(Smiles. He is right at home.)*

MR. HUGHES. Perhaps you'd like a pillow.

MIKE. No thanks. *(Then another smile)* Say, that's pretty good! You're a kidder, Mr. Hughes. Just like Jean, eh? I always like fathers that are regular guys.

*(*TEDDY *enters Right, holding the hand of* DOTTIE KIX-MILLER. DOTTIE *is brash, talkative, brightly dressed.* TEDDY *pauses at door.)*

TEDDY. *(With a gesture)* Hi, folks. *(Then an elaborately polite introduction)* Dottie, I want you to meet my father. Pop, this is Dottie Kixmiller.

DOTTIE. *(Crossing to* MR. HUGHES*)* Hi-ya, Mr. Hughes! *(Looks him over)* You don't look a bit like your son, but that's your advantage, I always say. *(Sees* MIKE*)* Hi, Mike. What you doin' here?

MIKE. How-ya, Dottie. I'm just—visiting.

MR. HUGHES. *(Crossing to stairs—speaking to* MIKE*)* I'll tell Jean you're here, Mr. Tisdale.

MIKE. Thanks, ole man.

*(*MR. HUGHES *looks back at him once, then goes.)*

TEDDY. *(Coming down Right, addressing* MIKE*)* Is that right? Did you come to see Jean—honest?

MIKE. I sure did.

DOTTIE. Wait till Ruth hears about this!

TEDDY. Well, I'll be darned. *(Sits in Right chair)* You know, that's funny. Jean never has any dates.

MIKE. You don't say?

DOTTIE. Not that *I'll* tell Ruth Coates, of course—but wait till she hears about it. I thought you two were all tied up in love knots.

MIKE. Not at all. *(To* TEDDY*)* So Jean doesn't go out much, eh?

TEDDY. Why, you must be the first date she's had—well, at least since that time she walked all over Wally Stevens' feet at one of the dances. That was the same night she spilled punch all over his palm beach suit. And on the way home she got him so mad and flustered by telling him what she didn't like about him that he smashed up his dad's car. *(Slight pause)* But I think you'll like her.

DOTTIE. Boy, I gotta see this dilly. She must be strictly on the side of angels for you to get swamped enough to toss Ruth Coates over.

*(*JEAN *comes down the stairs. She looks about the same except that she betrays some excitement now; her tears are gone.* TEDDY *rises and crosses to her at foot of stairs.* MIKE *rises and crosses to Center, facing* JEAN. DOTTIE *sits on arm of Right Center chair, watching.)*

TEDDY. Here she is. Say, Jean, I been telling Mike about you. I told him you don't ever have any dates.

JEAN. *(Angry—softly hissing)* Ted!

DOTTIE. So this is it! I'm stubblegasted! *(Sinks into chair, hand to forehead.)*

MIKE. Don't pay any attention to Teddy, Jean. *I* don't.

JEAN. *(Charmed)* Don't you?

DOTTIE. I wouldn't tell Ruth Coates anything—but somebody will. *(Rises)* Say Mike—there's something putrid about all this. What you got up your sleeve?

MIKE. Beat it, drip. Just because I'd never give you a tumble.

DOTTIE. *Me* a tumble? *(Insulted)* Why, I wouldn't walk as far as that window to see you drown yourself.

TEDDY. *(Very big)* Well, gotta go now. Gotta go. *(Crosses to* DOTTIE, *takes her arm, starts leading her to Right.)*

DOTTIE. When men say things like that, I wish I was a man myself. I'd lay you so flat— *(To* TEDDY*)* Stop pushing me. I don't like to be pushed. What is this?

*(*MIKE *crosses to foot of stairs.)*

TEDDY. It's getting late, Dottie. Gotta get you home before it gets too late—

DOTTIE. Late? Are you bats? The evening's just begun.

TEDDY. *(In a rush)* I get to bed early these days. Have to. In training. Come on, come on.

DOTTIE. In training for *what?*

TEDDY. *(Taking her arm again and pulling her into hall and off)* Training for graduation. Terrible ordeal. Terrible—

(The front DOOR slams. There is a pause. MIKE *turns to* JEAN.)*

MIKE. You know, Jean, I been watching you.

JEAN. *(Crossing down to sit on Left end of sofa)* You have?

MIKE. *(Following)* Yeah. In the halls, in class— you're in my Latin class, you know that? *(Sits in down Left chair.)*

JEAN. Yes, I know.

MIKE. *(Very charming and suave)* I don't pay any attention to what that brother of yours said. I kind of like girls that haven't had a lot of dates and don't think they know everything. I think it's an advantage.

JEAN. I'm glad you do.

MIKE. Don't you?

JEAN. I never have before.

MIKE. You don't mind my dropping in on you like this?

JEAN. I don't think so. I really like it.

MIKE. *(Rises and crosses in front of* JEAN *and sits beside her on sofa)* Because I know what it is to move into a strange town and not know anyone, to feel lonely. Especially if you have a hard time getting acquainted.—Take me now: I'm kind of shy about meeting people. *(He moves a little closer.)*

JEAN. *(Smiling)* I can hardly believe it.

MIKE. Sure you can—a girl like you. It's these slick chicks that can't understand a thing like that.

JEAN. *(A little sadly)* I'm not a slick chick, am I?

MIKE. Oh, I didn't mean that. You're okay. You got brains. These other gals, now—they're all fluff and molasses, fancy hair, spangles—you know: all fiddle and faddle, no grey stuff up here. *(Taps his head.)*

JEAN. I suppose the next thing you'll be telling me is: I have a mind like a man's.

MIKE. In a way, yeah. That's what I mean.

JEAN. That's always the highest compliment a man can pay a woman—*he* thinks.

MIKE. Take that Latin assignment now. I'd say that was too much of a good thing, wouldn't you?

JEAN. Oh, I don't know. I finished mine hours ago.

MIKE. I'm stymied.

JEAN. It's really easy.

MIKE. I just haven't got that kind of a mind, I guess. *(He moves even closer.)*

JEAN. Perhaps I could help you.

MIKE. Oh, now—I wouldn't want to presume on our friendship like that, Jean. *(Very close.)*

JEAN. I don't mind, Mike. *(Nervous, starts to rise.)*

MIKE. *(Placing a hand over hers)* Don't move now, Jean.

JEAN. No.—Why?

MIKE. I like talking with you.

JEAN. I thought you said— *(Swallows)* you wanted to do—

MIKE. *(Leaning close)* You're pretty, Jean. You're really pretty.

JEAN. *(Finishing lamely)* —Latin.

MIKE. *(In honeyed tones)* That can wait.

JEAN. Do you think it should?

MIKE. You know what I really came here to see you about, Jean?

JEAN. I'm beginning to wonder.

MIKE. About the Prom.

JEAN. *(Immediately excited)* The Prom!

MIKE. I 'been thinking a lot about you this week. And this evening I got an idea.

JEAN. Yes—?

MIKE. After the Prom every year, we usually have a big party.

JEAN. Do you mean you want me to go to the—

MIKE. And I was just thinking, you know—you being strange here and all—well, if your father and mother are on the beam, maybe we could have the party here.

JEAN. After the Prom, you mean?

MIKE. About eleven, say. Only last an hour or two. And I'll bring all the refreshments and all that. *(Rises and crosses to French windows)* You got a lot of room here and it's nice. And that way you could get acquainted with the right crowd and all.—We'd have it at my house only my father's a grouch. Ulcers, I think.

JEAN. *(Standing up—very happy)* I'd be very happy to go to the Prom with you, Mike.

MIKE. *(Startled, starts down to JEAN, gesturing)* I didn't—I mean—listen—

(SNAZZY MITCHELL enters at French windows. SNAZZY is a meek fellow, MIKE's age; he'd like to be like MIKE, but instead he is in many ways MIKE's opposite: small, gentle, with a naive, often confused

boyish expression. He wears a gob's hat, plaid shirt, unpressed slacks. He pauses in the French windows.)

SNAZZY. May I come in now?

(MIKE and JEAN turn. JEAN's expression is still one of bliss.)

MIKE. Come on in.
SNAZZY. I don't want to interrupt anything.
MIKE. I thought I told you to stay in the car.
SNAZZY. You did, Mike. But I got something to tell you. Confidential.
MIKE. Take off your hat.
SNAZZY. *(Snatches his hat from his head)* Sorry.
MIKE. Snazzy, this is Jean Hughes.
JEAN. How do you do, Snazzy?
SNAZZY. Hello. Pleased to meet you. Formally.
MIKE. *(To JEAN)* This is Snazzy Mitchell.
SNAZZY. They just call me that. My real name is Aloysius. *(Laughs through his nose, embarrassed.)*
MIKE. *(To JEAN)* Pardon me, Jean. *(Under his breath, threateningly, to SNAZZY)* When I say wait in the car, I mean wait in the car. You came prancing in just at the wrong time. Now beat it.
SNAZZY. But, Mike—
MIKE. G'wan, beat it.

(He takes SNAZZY by the shirt front and starts him toward French windows.)

SNAZZY. You'll be sorry, Mike. Listen! You don't want to be sorry. You'll just blame me in the end. *(As they get near windows)* Ruth just went by *(Then very loud)* Ruth Coates just went by outside.
MIKE. *(Releasing him)* She did?
SNAZZY. *(Straightening out his shirt and trying to regain a little dignity)* She saw me in the car and stopped and wanted to know where you were.
MIKE. What'd you tell her?

SNAZZY. I said I didn't know.

MIKE. What'd she say?

SNAZZY. She said I was a liar.

MIKE. *(Obviously in a hurry now—crossing to* JEAN*)* Well, Jean—it's all arranged, then. Okay? The party's set for here after the Prom. Right? *(Rubs hands together enthusiastically.)*

JEAN. I guess so, Mike. I think so. But—

MIKE. *(Taking her hand)* I've enjoyed this visit a lot, Jean—talking to a smart, sensible girl about serious things. It's a great change, believe me.

JEAN. Are you going, Mike?

MIKE. Yeah—I got to go now. I—

JEAN. What'll I wear to the Prom, Mike? Do you like yellow?

MIKE. Yellow—? Oh, yeah, I like yellow.

SNAZZY. *(Stepping in—loud)* Mike! Did you date her for the Prom?

MIKE. *(Grabbing* SNAZZY *by shirt again and hurrying him to Right)* Come on, Snazzy. And shut up.

JEAN. *(Quickly)* But, Mike—what about the Latin?

MIKE. You do it tonight and I'll see you before class tomorrow.

JEAN. But—all right, Mike.

MIKE. That's a sweetheart!

*(*MIKE *has propelled* SNAZZY *to the hall now. The front DOOR slams and* AMY *bursts in, meeting* MIKE *and* SNAZZY *at entrance to hall.* AMY *blocks their way; looks them over.)*

AMY. *(To* MIKE*)* Who are you—the bouncer?

MIKE. Out of the way, small fry.

AMY. *(To* SNAZZY*)* Why do you let this ape push you around like that?

SNAZZY. I don't. I mean—he doesn't exactly—

AMY. *(Brushing past them and into room)* I'd be ashamed of myself. *(Flops into Right Center chair; sprawls.)*

SNAZZY. *(Disentangling himself)* Lemme go, will you? *(Straightens his shirt again; pushes his shirt tail in. Crosses to face* AMY*)* I don't believe we've met, have we?

JEAN. Snazzy Mitchell, this is my kid sister—Amy.

SNAZZY. *(Intrigued)* Hello, Amy.

AMY. *(Meets his eye)* Hi there.

SNAZZY. Gosh, how'd I happen not to meet you before now?

AMY. *(Interested)* I don't pay any attention to boys —usually. They're goons.

SNAZZY. *(Deflated)* Oh.

AMY. *(Rising)* Only—

SNAZZY. *(In a rush)* Amy, look—I don't want you to think I'm fresh or anything and having just met you and your not knowing me and here we stand talking anyway—I mean any way you look at it it's almost bound to look sillier than it really is, if you know what I mean, but—

MIKE. Spill it, Romeo, and let's trot out of here.

SNAZZY. What I'm trying to say is—I don't know whether you date or not—and for all I know you may be going steady with someone—or maybe you're not even old enough and who knows what your mother would say, but—

*(*SNAZZY *and* AMY *are standing toe to toe, gazing deeply and seriously into each other's eyes.)*

AMY. *(Dreamily)* I'll go with you, Snazzy.

SNAZZY. What I mean to ask you is— *(Gets it)* You will? You'll go with me? *(Turns to* MIKE*)* She says she'll go with me! *(Laughs again, through his nose, embarrassed)* What do you know? *(Straightens himself up—surprise in his voice)* Well, that wasn't so hard. *(Laughs again)* It was *easy!* *(Places hat on head at jaunty angle, crosses to Right, exits.)*

MIKE. *(Shaking his head)* Whew! Smooth, isn't he? *(To* JEAN*)* Goodbye, Jean.

JEAN. Goodbye, Mike.

*(*MIKE *goes Right. The front door doesn't slam because no sooner does* MIKE *disappear than* SNAZZY

*bursts back into room from hall and goes breath-
lessly to* AMY.)

SNAZZY. *(Out of breath)* Maybe I forgot to mention
—I meant the Prom. I meant you'd go to the Prom
with me—that's what I was talking about, Amy.
AMY. Yes—I know—I will.
SNAZZY. *(Enthusiastically grabs both her arms, im-
mediately drops them)* I just wanted to make sure,
that's all. *(Goes to Right again; turns solemnly to room)*
Wheee! *(Disappears Right. DOOR slams.)*

(A pause. JEAN *sinks to sofa. Her thoughts are far
away.* AMY, *her eyes dreamily on the Right entrance where* SNAZZY *disappeared, crosses to sit
beside* JEAN *on sofa.* BOTH *sit staring silently for
a moment or two. Then:)*

JEAN. I can hardly believe it.
AMY. Me either.
JEAN. I never met anyone like him before.
AMY. Me either.
JEAN. *(In a breath)* Golly. Golly Moses!
AMY. I'm not even sure it means what I think it
means. *(A little angry)* What's he done to me anyway?
He doesn't have any right to make me feel this way.
JEAN. There're butterflies in my stomach.
AMY. Not butterflies. Bees. A whole buzzing swarm
of bees.
JEAN. And he doesn't even mind my glasses—or my
brains—or the awful way I look. He says he *likes* it.
Imagine that.
AMY. They're all goons, sure. He's a goon, too. No
denying it. Lets that guy paste him around. Can't even
complete a sentence. I bet he's a terrible dancer.
JEAN. He's a marvelous dancer.
AMY. *(Coming out of it a bit)* Who?
JEAN. Mike.
AMY. Oh—that homely.
JEAN. *(Sharply)* He's the best-looking boy in school.
AMY. *(Lost again)* And the way his eyes look—soft
and scared—

JEAN. *(In hushed tones)* Amy, you don't think—
AMY. *(A little sadly)* It looks that way.
JEAN. Imagine!
AMY. That's what it is, all right. Love.
JEAN. You too?
AMY. Me, too.
JEAN. But Amy, how do you know?
AMY. I know. That's all. I know. I don't feel good and I don't feel bad. I feel both— That's love.

(MR. and MRS. HUGHES come down the stairs, arm in arm. JEAN and AMY continue to stare ahead, unseeing.)

MRS. HUGHES. Mildred's sensitive, Jesse. Very sensitive.
MR. HUGHES. The whole family's "sensitive, very sensitive." So am I, but no one ever pays any attention to that.

(MR. and MRS. HUGHES have reached Center. They BOTH stare at JEAN and AMY, who do not see them.)

MRS. HUGHES. Amy, what are you doing here, dear? Did you say what I told you to? About our background?

(No answer.)

MR. HUGHES. *(Narrowing his eyes and bending down a bit toward JEAN and AMY)* Hello. *(No answer)* I say—hello. *(Turning to MRS. HUGHES)* Harriet, maybe they're sick.
MRS. HUGHES. Nonsense.
MR. HUGHES. They act just like they did when they had the mumps.
AMY. *(From a great distance)* You wouldn't understand, Daddy.
MR. HUGHES. Well, she can still talk. That's encouraging. *(Still looking at them, crosses down Left)* Jean —you look like you've seen a ghost.

JEAN. Not exactly.

MRS. HUGHES. *(Searching)* What's become of my book? *(Picks up the book* JEAN *had been reading;* MR. HUGHES *had left it in Right Center chair)* "A Psychological Study of—" *(She looks up)* Jesse, is this where you get all those silly ideas of yours? *(Sits in Right Center chair.)*

AMY. *(Rising)* Pardon me.

(Crosses slowly and deliberately to the stairs, her mind still in greener pastures. She starts up the stairs—very slowly. MR. and MRS. HUGHES watch. She disappears.)

MR. HUGHES. That's the slowest she's walked since she was eleven months old.

JEAN. *(Rising)* I have some—uh—some Latin to do. *(She also crosses to stairs slowly.)*

MR. HUGHES. I thought you did your Latin, Jean.

JEAN. Yes— This is some *other* Latin.

MR. HUGHES. Well, as long as you feel all right, Jean.

JEAN. *(Pausing on stairs, turning to face them)* By the way—we're going to have a party here Saturday night. After the Prom.

MR. HUGHES. Here?

MRS. HUGHES. Isn't that nice, dear? Be sure to invite—

(Before she can finish the front DOOR slams and TEDDY appears at Right. With him is another girl. She is handsome and dignified, about TEDDY's age. TEDDY holds her hand. JEAN pauses on the stairs.)

TEDDY. *(With a wave of his hand)* Hi, folks!

MR. HUGHES. Hello, Teddy. Glad to see you again, Miss Kixmiller.

TEDDY. Pop—this isn't Miss Kixmiller. This is Maryrosalie Vogulhut. *(Bringing her to Center)* This is my mother, Rosalie. And my father. And my sister, Jean.

MRS. HUGHES. How do you do, dear?

JEAN. Hello.

MR. HUGHES. *(Baffled)* Maryrosalie Vogulhut. Sorry—for a minute I thought you were—someone else. Sit down, won't you?

TEDDY. Oh, that's all right. Maryrosalie understands. *(But MARYROSALIE only smiles. TEDDY leads her to chair down Right; she sits; he stands by her)* Anybody can make a mistake. Can't they, Maryrosalie?

(MARYROSALIE smiles and nods; doesn't speak; arranges her skirt carefully and just sits there, silent and pleasant.)

MR. HUGHES. *(After a dead pause—sits in chair down Left)* Have you lived in Butterfield all your life?

(To this MARYROSALIE smiles and nods. MR. HUGHES is mystified.)

TEDDY. I just wanted Maryrosalie to meet all of you, you know.

MRS. HUGHES. *(To MARYROSALIE)* Have you been having a good time?

(MARYROSALIE nods and smiles again. MR. and MRS. HUGHES exchange glances.)

TEDDY. I always have a good time with Maryrosalie.

MR. HUGHES. *(Pointedly)* You do? What do you *talk* about?

TEDDY. *(Blandly)* Life.

MR. HUGHES. *(Defeated)* Oh.

TEDDY. *(Crossing to Center)* By the way, Pop— what time is it?

MR. HUGHES. *(Consulting his watch)* It's ten after nine, Teddy. Why?

TEDDY. *(Turning to MARYROSALIE)* Well, Maryrosalie—getting late.

(MARYROSALIE gives him a puzzled look, startled. He crosses to her; very gallantly offers his arm. MARYROSALIE takes his arm; rises. MR. HUGHES rises.)

MR. HUGHES. Goodbye, Maryrosalie.

TEDDY. *(As they go out at Right)* Don't go right to bed now, folks. I'll be back soon.

MR. HUGHES. *(Almost a plea)* Teddy—no—not another one— *(Crosses to hall and exits. We hear him:)* I'm going to bed right now! Right this second!

JEAN. *(Comes down the stairs and crosses to French windows)* I don't want to go to my room just yet. *(Leaning in window)* I think I'll go for a long walk in the moonlight.

MRS. HUGHES *(Who has opened the book and begun to read)* This is absolutely the silliest book I have ever read in my life.

(MR. HUGHES *enters at Right. With him is* RUTH COATES. RUTH *is a Senior, too—quite an attractive one. She is well dressed. She is pert, not unintelligent, extremely popular.)*

MR. HUGHES. I met this young lady on the doorstep.

JEAN. Oh—hello, Ruth.

RUTH. Hello.

(MR. HUGHES *stays Right.* RUTH *comes to Center.* JEAN *joins her there.)*

JEAN. Mother, I'd like for you to know Ruth Coates.

RUTH. *(To* MRS. HUGHES, *who rises)* How do you do, Mrs. Hughes? I really came to see you. At least that's the excuse for my visit.

JEAN. And you've met my father.

RUTH. Yes. He shouted into my face on the porch. He said he was going to bed. Right away.

MR. HUGHES. And so I am. *(Crosses to stairs)* I'm glad to have met you, Miss Coates. Excuse me. *(Starts up the stairs)* If Teddy comes back with another girl, tell him she'll have to meet this part of his family at a later date.

MRS. HUGHES. Jesse, you can't sleep this early.

MR. HUGHES. I'm going to read your book, dear— the one about the great lover. Our son seems to be one;

I might as well get to know something about how they click. *(Disappears.)*

MRS. HUGHES. *(To* RUTH*)* Sit down, dear.

RUTH. Thank you. *(Sits on sofa.* JEAN *stands behind sofa)* Mother said she'd come to call soon, but meanwhile she wants me to extend an invitation to attend a meeting of the Clover Club on Saturday night. She'll drop by to make it official.

MRS. HUGHES. *(Sitting again)* The Clover Club! Saturday night? No, I'm not a bit busy Saturday night. Tell her I'd be delighted, utterly delighted!

RUTH. Mother's been President for ten or twelve years. In a way she *is* the Clover Club.

JEAN. But, Mother—on Saturday I'm having the party. Remember—I told you.

MRS. HUGHES. Well, of course, dear—but you don't need me. I'd just be in the way. Your father's a perfectly capable chaperone.

RUTH. Is that Mike Tisdale's party you're speaking of?

JEAN. Yes, it is. Mike's and—mine. We'd love to have you, Ruth.

RUTH. Oh, I'll be here.

JEAN. Good.

RUTH. With Mike.

JEAN. With—!!

RUTH. *(Not unpleasantly)* I go every place with Mike.

JEAN. *(It has begun to dawn)* I see. *(Then crossing to Center—to* MRS. HUGHES*)* Mother, don't you have some little book to read yourself?

MRS. HUGHES. No, dear—all I'm reading is that crazy psychological—

JEAN. *(Pointedly)* Upstairs, I mean.

MRS. HUGHES. I can't read in bed, Jean. You know that. It gives me headaches. *(To* RUTH*)* I get the most awful headaches. I think I need glasses, really. Like Jean. But I'd hate to wear them. They make you look—

JEAN. *(Ready to burst now)* I know how terrible they make me look, Mother. Let's not discuss it now, shall we?

Mrs. Hughes. *(Rising, book in hand)* Have I hurt you, Jean? I'm sorry. I just say whatever drops into my head. I shouldn't.

Jean. *(Hurt and desperate)* It's all right, Mother. I think I hear Daddy calling you.

Mrs. Hughes. I'll go, dear. *(Starts toward stairs)* And thanks for dropping in, Ruth.

Ruth. You're welcome.

Mrs. Hughes. *(Disappears up stairs)* You know what I'm going to do for penance, Jean? I'm going to read this terrible book from cover to cover—if it kills me.

Jean. She's really nice, you know. Just thoughtless.

Ruth. I can see that.

Jean. *(Going to stand at Right end of sofa)* Did Mike tell you about the party?

Ruth. No. I knew he was here tonight—and I put the rest together. *(Rising)* You see, Jean—Mike wanted me to have the party at my house.

Jean. Why didn't you?

Ruth. My father wouldn't let me. *(Crosses to Right —in front of Jean, who turns to watch Ruth)* In fact, he ordered Mike off the premises as soon as he brought it up. *(Turns to face Jean)* Mike's parties are something!

Jean. What do you mean by that?

Ruth. Well, the last time he threw a party at my house, it was the Fourth of July. He burned our summer house to the ground.

Jean. I don't believe it. He isn't like that. And I don't like to hear you talking about him like this.

Ruth. Listen—I've known Mike since we both went to kindergarten together. He's quite a fella. I may even be in love with him, but that's my hard luck. He was expelled from kindergarten for biting the teacher. In grade school, when the other boys made spit balls, Mike threw ball bearings.

Jean. You're making it up. You know he has a date with me for the Prom and you're jealous.

Ruth. *(Starts to Right)* Take it that way if you like.

JEAN. *(Stepping after her)* You came here just to tell me this?

RUTH. *(Turning to face* JEAN*)* In a way I did. Also, I thought I'd like to get acquainted.

JEAN. *(Icily)* Well, we're acquainted. *(Turns and crosses to Left—bewildered, in pain.)*

RUTH. *(Losing her temper, crosses swiftly after* JEAN*)* And maybe I'm doing you a favor.

JEAN. Never mind, thanks. I don't need you.

RUTH. You're in Mike's Latin class, aren't you?

JEAN. *(Her spirits roused)* What of it?

RUTH. Has he asked you to do his Latin yet? Has he?

JEAN. No!

RUTH. And now you're lying.

JEAN. Don't call me a liar! *(The TELEPHONE rings.* JEAN *crosses to desk and* RUTH *crosses down Left; stands tapping her foot. Into telephone—not very pleasantly barking)* Hughes residence— Hold the line. I'll call her. *(Goes to stairs; calls)* Mildred! *Mildred!* Telephone.

MILDRED. *(Upstairs)* I'm coming.

JEAN. *(Returning immediately to* RUTH, *fight still in her)* Now, where were we?

RUTH. You said I called you a liar.

JEAN. Well, didn't you?

RUTH. If he hasn't asked you, he will.

JEAN. Asked me what?

RUTH. To do his Latin!

MILDRED. *(Comes down the stairs. She wears a housecoat and has a towel wrapped around her head. She is very tired. As she enters)* Who is it?

JEAN. A boy. He sounded silly. Charles something-or-other.

MILDRED. *(Reaching telephone—thrilled)* Charles Collier! *(Takes up telephone)* Hello— Why, yes, Charles. How are *you?*

(The tempo picks up and gathers speed to Curtain.)

RUTH. I don't want to stand and argue with you. I

just don't want to see you get all balled up, then hurt.

JEAN. You're pretty sure of yourself, aren't you?

RUTH. Fairly so—with Mike.

MILDRED. *(Into telephone)* I'm fine, Charles, just *fine*— Saturday night? Let's see—

JEAN. Because of your looks, I suppose—and your clothes. Because you're popular with the boys and—

RUTH. Let's not go into my virtues.

JEAN. Mike's the first boy ever treated me like a human being. He's the first boy I didn't want to laugh at.

MILDRED. Shhhhh! *(Then into telephone)* No, I have a little sort of date, but nothing I can't break, Charles.

AMY. *(Wearing a robe over pajamas, comes tearing down the stairs—not at all the starry-eyed girl who went upstairs)* Who's the phone for? *(Pauses on stairs.)*

MILDRED. *(Holding hand over phone)* Please—for Heaven's sake. I can't hear a thing. *(Into phone)* A little disturbance on the line, I think—

RUTH. If he asked you to go to the Prom, Jean—he's going to take you. Even if he has had a date with me.

JEAN. And don't start being nice to me. I hate to have people be nice to me. It makes me see seven thousand shades of purple!!

(In the confusion the front DOOR has opened and TEDDY is there again. This time the girl whose hand he holds is HOPE SHUTTLEWORTH. HOPE is the gushing type, a little simpering, in looks a doll.)

TEDDY. *(As before)* Hi, folks! *(A pause—brief)* This is Hope Shuttleworth.

HOPE. *(Going to RUTH)* I'll bet you're Mildred. I've heard so much about you from Teddy. You go to college, don't you?

MILDRED. *(Holding hand over telephone—very loud)* Shut up!

HOPE. *(Startled)* My— Who's that?

TEDDY. That's Mildred.

MILDRED. *(Into telephone—with glares to the room in general)* I'm so sorry, Charles. There's so much confusion here. *(Through her teeth)* Everyone is so gay—No—gay—gay!

AMY. *(To* HOPE*)* I'm Amy.

HOPE. *(To* RUTH*)* Then I guess you're Jean.

RUTH. I should say not!

JEAN. I'm Jean.

TEDDY. Where's Pop? Say, don't tell me he went to bed.

MILDRED. *(Into telephone)* I think so, too, Charles. Definitely!

MIKE. *(The front DOOR opens again and from the hall emerge: first* MIKE *giving directions)* Now everything's all right, Officer. He's home now in the bosom of his family and it's all— *(To the room)* Stand back, everybody.

(Then in comes the policeman, MR. LIPSCOMB, *carrying an inert* SNAZZY. LIPSCOMB *struggles toward the sofa and places* SNAZZY *there; straightens up, dusts his hands. As soon as he enters,* AMY *dashes wildly toward* SNAZZY *and kneels before him on floor. He is stretched out on sofa.)*

LIPSCOMB. *(Irascibly)* I might have known it'd end up here.

AMY. Snazzy, speak to me! Snazzy—!

LIPSCOMB. *(To* MIKE*)* You sure you don't want me to get an ambulance?

MIKE. No. Just a fainting spell. Has 'em all the time. His ole man knows what to do.

(At this inopportune time MR. HUGHES *comes down the stairs, a dressing gown over his trousers and shirt, his hair mussed.* LIPSCOMB *sees him on stairs and crosses to meet him.)*

LIPSCOMB. It's all right, Mr. Hughes. Just another one of your kids. The one that faints. *(Turns to glare at* TEDDY, *who has started to speak.)*

TEDDY. But Snazzy's not—

LIPSCOMB. The one that faints, not the other crazy one. (*Leering at* TEDDY, *then turns to* MR. HUGHES, *who is flabbergasted and silent*) In a way I feel sorry for you, Mister. (*Turns to* MIKE) And you—watch your speed. I don't care who you're taking to what hospital. (*Stomps to hall at Right and goes.*)

MR. HUGHES. (*Baffled, crosses to Center*) What the devil is all this?

MIKE. (*Blandly*) It's all right, Mr. Hughes. Just a little joke. You see, I was—well, going too fast—in this direction—and that copper stops me—and so I told Snazzy here to play like he'd fainted and I was taking him home—

AMY. (*Kneeling beside* SNAZZY, *who doesn't open his eyes*) If he fainted, why didn't you take him to *his* house? Don't you think we better get a doctor?

MIKE. (*Playing it up*) He didn't *really* faint. And since we weren't going toward his house, well—I had to say we were going *somewhere*—and this is the first place I thought of— (*Sees* RUTH *for first time. His expression changes, his good-humored and ingratiating mask falls. In a different voice*) —Oh, hello, Ruth.

RUTH. (*With an expression of pained acceptance*) Hello, Drip. (*Through her teeth*) So this is the first place you thought of—

MR. HUGHES. (*Angered*) I never heard of anything so— (*Bends over* SNAZZY) Wake up! (*Shakes* SNAZZY) Wake up, you. (*To* MIKE) What's his name?

AMY. Snazzy.

MR. HUGHES. (*Distastefully*) Snazzy? (*Then to* SNAZZY) Hey, Snazzy—get up! (*Examines his eyes.*)

MIKE. (*Still worried about* RUTH'S *expression, crosses to her*) Well, gee, Ruth—you didn't want me to get pinched, did you?

RUTH. I think a few years in jail would do you good.

MR. HUGHES. This boy's really fainted!

AMY. (*Wailing*) Snazzy!

MILDRED. (*Who has been talking in an undertone below the above, hangs up and faces them*) I think you're the most horrid group of characters I have ever seen in my life! *(Stomps toward the stairs and exits during following.)*

MIKE. *(Worried)* Maybe that ride was too much for him? We traveled pretty fast—with a police escort. Almost hit a street car.

(SNAZZY stirs. ALL watch. Then he opens his eyes, one at a time; half sits up.)

AMY. Snazzy! Snazzy, *darling*—are you all right? Say something.

SNAZZY. Don't tell me. I know what happened. We hit a street car. We hit— *(To MR. HUGHES)* Am I all right, Doctor?

MR. HUGHES. *(Disgusted by now)* I'm not a doctor. Don't you recognize me? I'm your father.

SNAZZY. My f-f-f-f-f——? My *father?!*

JEAN. *(Rushing to MIKE)* Mike, are you taking Ruth to the Prom? That's all I want to know—

MIKE. *(Hedging)* Well, I—

JEAN. Answer yes or no!

RUTH. *(Coming up behind JEAN)* Answer her, Big Shot. I'm on her side. *(WARN Curtain.)*

MIKE. You are? Well—yes, I guess I am. I mean—

JEAN. *(Angry)* Then you've been lying! You don't like girls with grey stuff up here. *(Taps her head)* It's the spangles—the fiddle and the faddle, after all. Well, all right!

HOPE. *(To TEDDY)* Is that your sister?

JEAN. *(Ripping off her glasses)* I'll show you! The whole lot of you! *(She hurls her glasses at the wall where they break—or to floor. Then to RUTH)* And I don't want you on my side—anybody on my side—but if it's fluff and molasses they want, I can give it to them!

HOPE. What's the matter with her, anyway?

JEAN. *(Turns on heel and clicks determinedly to stairs; turns to room)* Watch my dust! From now on, little sister sizzles! *(Tears upstairs.)*

SNAZZY. Where am I?

AMY. I'm here, Snazzy.

RUTH. *(To MIKE)* Now see what you've done—you and your irresponsible tricks! Your darned fool gags! You've upset this whole family until—

SNAZZY. *(Sits up—plaintively)* What's all the yelling about?

MR. HUGHES. *(Pushes SNAZZY over and sits beside him on sofa)* Move over, Son.

SNAZZY. What's all the commotion?

MR. HUGHES. Never mind, Son. You're in the family now. You'll have to get used to these things.

MRS. HUGHES. *(Appears on stairs, her hair in curlers and wearing a house coat. Peering down from stairs)* Jesse—Jesse—do we have company?

(But we never hear his reply because the

CURTAIN HAS FALLEN QUICKLY

ACT TWO

SCENE: *The same.*

TIME: *Eight o'clock the following Friday evening.*

AT RISE: MR. HUGHES *is stretched out comfortably on the sofa, a newspaper under his feet. The LIGHTS are turned on. A moment passes. Then the dining-room door opens quickly and AMY, wearing a housecoat and carrying a freshly pressed evening gown, her hair in curlers, dashes pell-mell into the room and up the stairs—noisily. MR. HUGHES doesn't stir. Another very brief pause. Then the front DOOR opens and MRS. HUGHES, wearing a frilly hat and dress, enters from Right. She is in a dither.*

MRS. HUGHES. *(Crossing quickly to stairs)* I'm late, I'm late, I'm late. *(Sees MR. HUGHES)* Hello, dear. *(Rushes on without his answer)* I've been at the Auxiliary all afternoon and Mrs. Coates is coming in a very few minutes to take me to the Clover Club. *(On the stairs)* You'll be nice to her, won't you, dear? *(Disappears.)*

MR. HUGHES. *(Without lifting his head)* I'll kiss her once on each ear.

(Immediately the DOORBELL rings. MR. HUGHES rises, goes Right, disappears. While he is gone, AMY's voice is heard from upstairs:)

AMY. *(Off)* Teddy's in the bathroom again! He's combed his hair seven times!

44

(A DOOR slams upstairs—loud. As Mr. Hughes *returns from the hall at Right,* Mildred *dashes down the stairs, wearing an evening gown and bedroom slippers. She is well groomed.* Mr. Hughes *carries a corsage box from florist's.)*

Mildred. *(On stairs)* Is that for me?

Mr. Hughes. *(A trifle sadly)* No. This is for Jean. *(Places box on table and resumes his place on sofa during following:)*

Mildred. That Charles Collier had better send flowers! *(Turns and goes swiftly up stairs again.)*

Jean. *(Wearing housecoat, bedroom slippers, and with a towel around her head, her glasses still in place, enters from kitchen; she also carries a freshly pressed evening gown—which looks a bit incongruous in her hands. As she crosses to stairs)* Evening, Daddy.

Mr. Hughes. Jean—

Jean. *(Pausing at foot of stairs)* Yes—?

Mr. Hughes. The box on the table is for you.

Jean. *(Crossing to it curiously)* For me—?

Mr. Hughes. From some swain, no doubt.

Jean. *(Who has been opening box)* Flowers. *(Holds them up)* Carnations. *(Puts them against her)* Isn't Tommy sweet?

Mr. Hughes. *(Startled)* Tommy?! *(Sits up)* Tommy? Maybe I'm wrong but I thought you were going to the Prom with that fast-talking Romeo that hits everybody on the back.

Jean. Oh—you mean Mike. No—no, that was some kind of a misunderstanding. Tommy's a kind of Physics genius—but awfully nice. He asked me because I'm the only one who got an A-plus in Physics. That's his favorite subject.

Mr. Hughes. That's the best reason for a date I ever heard. You can discuss relativity while you dance.

Jean. Tommy's sweet—but not like Mike.

Mr. Hughes. I like that Tommy already.

Jean. *(Reproving)* Daddy! *(Sits beside him)* I don't love Tommy, though.

MR. HUGHES. Jean—you're not going to tell me you're in love.

JEAN. It must be that. I can't conjugate any word but love in Latin anymore. *(Begins to do so dreamily)* Amo— *(She goes on with it.)*

MR. HUGHES. *(Interrupting)* All right. I'm convinced. Who's Mike taking?

JEAN. Ruth Coates. But it's more habit than anything.

MR. HUGHES. *(Tenderly)* I just hope you're not building up to an awful let-down, Jean.

JEAN. *(Rising)* You'll treat him nice at the party tonight, won't you, Daddy? *(Crosses to stairs.)*

MR. HUGHES. What *am* I all of a sudden? Don't I treat everybody nice? Have you ever seen me eat peas with a knife?

(A DOOR slams upstairs and AMY's voice comes down:)

AMY. *(Off)* At last!

(As JEAN goes up stairs, TEDDY comes down. He is dressed for the Prom—tuxedo if desired. JEAN and TEDDY meet. He gives her a long look. Then:)

TEDDY. Gosh, you look awful.

JEAN. You shut up! *(Exits swiftly.)*

TEDDY. *(Continuing down stairs, puzzled, looking after JEAN)* What did I say?

MR. HUGHES. Never mind, Son.

TEDDY. Well, am I slick or am I slick? *(At Center)* Boy, I'm gonna have to be pretty slick tonight, Pop. I'm on a spot. *(Sits beside MR. HUGHES.)*

MR. HUGHES. Is that unusual?

TEDDY. This is a tough spot—about the size of a pin head. I got three dates tonight. Three—count 'em. Dottie, Maryrosalie, Hope— I can't see where they all got the idea, anyway.

MR. HUGHES. I imagine you gave it to them, Teddy. *(A thought strikes him)* Wait a minute! *(Hand to head)* Wait just a minute!—Do you mean to tell me you've got three dates for the Prom and then you're going to bring all three to the party here afterward?

TEDDY. *(Shrugs)* I wish I could see a way out of it. —Still, I'd hate to have to choose. I like 'em all.

MR. HUGHES. And I'm supposed to be chaperone. *(Rises)* Teddy, if those females start fighting over you, we're *both* on a spot. *(Crosses Right, thinking over the dire possibilities.)*

TEDDY. *(Pleased)* Gee, do you think they might *fight* over me? *(Rises)* Say, that's super. *(Grinning)* I never had any girls fighting over me before.

MR. HUGHES. *(Turning to face TEDDY. Speaks slowly)* I don't know why I've got this feeling I've got— but something tells me I'm going to get caught right smack in the middle of this whole crazy business.

(The DOORBELL rings. MR. HUGHES goes into hall. TEDDY, very pleased, is thinking over his popularity at Center. AMY appears briefly on stairs; calls down:)

AMY. If that's for me, tell him to wait! *(Disappears.)*

(MR. HUGHES follows MRS. VICTORIA COATES into room from Right. MRS. COATES is dignity personified; she doesn't carry a lorgnette, but you feel she'd be more comfortable with one. She has a way of looking down her nose. Her manner is pleasant, however; at least she does try to make it so— not always with success.)

MRS. COATES. Thank you, Mr. Hughes.

MR. HUGHES. Won't you sit down, Mrs. Coates?

MRS. COATES. *(Trying to decide on a place)* Thank you.

MR. HUGHES. May I present our son—Theodore.— Ted, I'd like for you to meet Mrs. Coates. *(Crosses to down Right.)*

TEDDY. Can that Theodore stuff, Pop. *(To MRS.*

COATES—*with an ingratiating grin*) I'm Teddy. Are you Ruth's mother?

MRS. COATES. *(Sitting finally in Right Center chair)* Yes, I am.

TEDDY. I know Ruth. She doesn't look much like you, does she?

MRS. COATES. Some people think she does.

TEDDY. Ruth's kind of good-looking.

(MRS. COATES' *mouth goes shut and her smile fades. To make things worse,* AMY *comes dashing down the stairs, wearing her evening gown now but still on the rowdy side.*)

AMY. *(As she comes)* I thought you were never coming— *(Stops as she sees* MRS. COATES*)* Oh. *(Wide-eyed)* Pardon me. *(Turns and starts back up stairs in same rush)* I thought you were Snazzy! *(Disappears.)*

MRS. COATES. She thought I was what?

MR. HUGHES. That's our daughter, Mrs. Coates. She's a sophomore in high school and I'm afraid too buoyant. I apologize.

MRS. COATES. *(Unbending)* Well, one never can be sure about children, can one? They learn. It takes time.

TEDDY. Pardon me, Mrs. Coates—I have to go now. Have a date, you know. Several of them. *(Crosses to* MR. HUGHES.*)*

MRS. COATES. Of course, Theodore.

TEDDY. Pop, I wanted to talk to you about something else. My allowance doesn't seem to go as far in Butterfield as it did in Sheridan City. I don't know why.

MR. HUGHES. I do— In Sheridan City you had only one girl.

TEDDY. Maybe. Anyway, Pop, I gotta get flowers for them. You understand a thing like that. I imagine you bought flowers for a girl once or twice yourself.

MR. HUGHES. I bought a great many flowers for girls. But always out of my current allowance.

TEDDY. Yeah, I forgot. You must have been quite a Joe.

MR. HUGHES. I wouldn't say—

TEDDY. French coquettes, socking policemen — (*Clicks his tongue and grins.*)

MR. HUGHES. (*Quickly digging into his pocket and pushing three or four bills into* TEDDY's *hand*) Oh, for Pete's sake! Here—

TEDDY. Thanks, Pop. You won't regret it. (*Smoothes out the crumpled bills and turns to* MRS. COATES—*again the man-of-the-world*) It's been a pleasure meeting you, Mrs. Coates. (*A little bow, very charming.*)

MRS. COATES. Thank you.

TEDDY. (*To* MRS. HUGHES) And I suppose I'll be seeing you before the evening's over.

MR. HUGHES. I'm afraid so.

TEDDY. (*As he exits Right*) 'Bye.

(*The front DOOR slams after him. A pause.* MR. HUGHES *seats himself in the down Right chair.* MRS. COATES *turns to him.*)

MRS. COATES. Mr. Hughes, as you probably know, I'm President of the Clover Club in Butterfield. It's just a small group, but of course we think a great deal of it.

MR. HUGHES. Of course you do.

MRS. COATES. Well, what I'm trying to say is: I think, from all I've been able to learn, that your wife would be a valuable addition to our group. She's enterprising, helpful, ambitious—all the things we are, all of us. And her family background is of the best, as you know.

MR. HUGHES. I know.

MRS. COATES. But naturally you do. You looked into it before you were married, I've no doubt of it.

MR. HUGHES. No, I didn't— But I've heard a lot about it since.

MRS. COATES. However—and I hope you'll understand, Mr. Hughes—I haven't been able to ascertain whether *your* family is the one that settled in Rhode Island and then distinguished itself in the Revolution, or whether it's the one that built up a fortune in rum and spices, only to have the Democrats take it away from you. Perhaps you can enlighten me.

MR. HUGHES. *(Half-smiling)* Mrs. Coates, this is going to come as a surprise to you, but my people, as far back as we've been able to go, were mostly coal-miners. One branch did go in for vaudeville for a while, but most of them stuck to the pits.

MRS. COATES. *(Hoping against hope)* The coal-mining interests in England, you mean?

MR. HUGHES. No—Pennsylvania. And their only interest seemed to be in getting as much coal out as possible, because they were paid pretty poorly and every ounce counted.

MRS. COATES. *(Weakly)* You don't say?

MR. HUGHES. *(Rising)* Mrs. Coates, I'm afraid you'll find we're just a typical American family. Not an aristocrat in a carload.

MRS. COATES. You don't say?

MR. HUGHES. But you won't find us apologizing for it. At least not this member of the family. *(Crosses to down Left.)*

MRS. COATES. Of course not. I wouldn't want you to. It's just that in the Clover Club we have to be *so* careful.

MR. HUGHES. *(Turning to face her)* Well, you're perfectly safe with Mrs. Hughes. Her family tree's a yard wide and several miles tall—and the only one who was ever hanged on it was an uncle who took too great an interest in his neighbor's horses. *(Smiles)* —Shall I call Mrs. Hughes?

MRS. HUGHES. *(At this point MRS. HUGHES appears on the stairs. She has changed clothes and is now a bit nervous)* Oh, I'm so sorry, Mrs. Coates. Amy *just* told me—just this very minute! I hope I haven't kept you waiting. *(Now at foot of stairs.)*

MRS. COATES. I haven't minded at all. Mr. Hughes has kept me amused.

MRS. HUGHES. *(With a look toward MR. HUGHES— apprehensive)* Has he?

MRS. COATES. He's a very witty man, really. *Very* witty! *(Rising)* —Are you ready?

MRS. HUGHES. Yes, all ready. *(Crosses to MR. HUGHES)* Have a good time, dear. And take care of the children. I'm sure they won't be any trouble. *(Over her shoulder to* Mrs. Coates*)* They're such very well-behaved children.

Mrs. Coates. I met two of them. *(Enough said.)*

Mr. Hughes. Goodbye, Harriet.

(Mrs. Hughes *and* Mrs. Coates *go to hall at Right.)*

Mrs. Coates. It's been a pleasure, Mr. Hughes.

Mr. Hughes. It has, indeed. I hope not too upsetting a one for you.

Mrs. Coates. Not at all. Goodbye. *(Goes into hall.)*

Mrs. Hughes. *(To* Mr. Hughes—*angrily but under her breath)* Jesse, what have you been telling her?

Mr. Hughes. *(Levelly)* I answered her questions, that's all.

Mrs. Hughes. You didn't mention Uncle Josh, did you?

Mr. Hughes. I may have.

Mrs. Hughes. Jesse! That black sheep!

Mr. Hughes. *(Crossing to her)* Harriet, we haven't time to talk about it now—but I'm worried. You and I are going to have to have a long talk sometime—sometime soon. *(Kisses her lightly)* Goodbye.

Mrs. Hughes. When I get time, Jesse. Maybe. What do we have to talk about? *(Exits Right.)*

(Mr. Hughes, *frowning, goes to sit thoughtfully on the Right end of sofa. After a moment* Mildred *appears on stairs.)*

Mildred. Daddy—have my flowers come yet?

Mr. Hughes. No, Mildred—not yet.

Mildred. A banker's son, imagine! You don't think he's—well—

Mr. Hughes. Too tight-fisted to buy flowers, you mean? He might be.

Mildred. No, he's not! He's wonderful! Wait till you meet him!

Mr. Hughes. I'm waiting, Mildred.

Mildred. You'll love him. *(Disappears.)*

(MR. HUGHES *takes out pipe, lights it, shakes his head, trying to make something come clear to him. Then the DOORBELL rings again. Before he can rise, AMY tears down the stairs, flies to hall, disappears. We hear her voice:)*

AMY. *(In hall)* Oh—it's you. *(Drooping, disappointed, she returns)* Come on in. *(Shakes her head and goes to stairs and up.)*

(TOMMY KING *enters at Right. TOMMY is a Senior— but with a difference. Serious and shy. He is slender and not quite at ease in his best suit or tuxedo. He has a quick, fleeting smile which is immediately ingratiating. He has difficulty keeping his hair from tumbling forward. Until he is put at his ease, his feet have a way of getting tangled with each other and with furniture. MR. HUGHES rises.)*

MR. HUGHES. How do you do?

TOMMY. Hello.

MR. HUGHES. Is your name Collier?

TOMMY. No, sir. King.

MR. HUGHES. *(At a loss for a moment)* I see. Well, sit down.

TOMMY. Okay. *(Sits in down Right chair.)*

MR. HUGHES. *(Hesitantly)* You're not—Tommy— are you?

TOMMY. *(Brightening)* That's right. I'm Tommy.

MR. HUGHES. Jean received your flowers.

TOMMY. Just carnations. *(Smiles)* All I could afford.

MR. HUGHES. *(Warming up to the boy)* They were good looking. I always liked carnations.

TOMMY. *(Simply)* She deserves orchids.

MR. HUGHES. *(Rises and crosses to Right)* Tommy, shake hands.

TOMMY. Okay.—Why?

MR. HUGHES. *(Shaking TOMMY's hand)* I just thought they'd stopped turning out boys like you. I want to make sure you're real.

TOMMY. (Disentangling his hand) I don't like for people to make fun of me.

MR. HUGHES. (Abashed) I'm not making fun. I mean it. If you only knew— (Crosses to Left again, shaking head.)

TOMMY. Okay.—It's just that some people make fun of me all the time. And one of these days—

(The DOORBELL interrupts. MR. HUGHES starts to cross to Right.)

MR. HUGHES. I'm head doorman here tonight.

(But he doesn't reach hall; the outside DOOR is heard to open and MIKE appears at Right. He is snappily dressed and wears a wide smile.)

MIKE. Hello, hello! (Crosses to meet MR. HUGHES at Center) How-ya, Mr. H, ole man? Say, you don't look so fit tonight. Something bothering you?

MR. HUGHES. To be absolutely truthful—yes.

MIKE. Too bad. Ulcers, probably. My old man has them. (Sees TOMMY) Well, if it isn't Einstein! (Crosses to Right) Who let you out of the laboratory, Steinie?

TOMMY. (Rising) Listen, Tisdale—

(But he doesn't finish because SNAZZY, also dressed for the Prom, appears at Right.)

SNAZZY. (In a squeaky voice) May I come in now?

MIKE. (To SNAZZY) Sure, Snazz. Come on in and meet everyone. (Crossing again to MR. HUGHES near Center) —Everything all set for the party, Mr. H? (Crosses up to windows and looks out) Pretty fine night out there. (Takes a deep breath) Ought to be some party!

SNAZZY. (Entering sheepishly) Hello, Tommy. Hello, Mr. Hughes.

MR. HUGHES. (Seating himself at Left end of sofa) Don't be so bashful, Son. I thought you were one of the family.

SNAZZY. *(Desperate to explain)* I'm awfully sorry about that, Mr. Hughes. You see, Mike got that idea and—

MIKE. *(Gets a thought, interrupts, crossing to TOMMY)* Say! I get it now! You're taking Jean. *(Laughs)* That's a hot one!

SNAZZY. *(Continuing to MR. HUGHES)* And you know Mike's ideas. I didn't want to pretend to be your son that night. I don't *want* to be your son. I got a date with your daughter.

MR. HUGHES. Which one?

SNAZZY. Amy, of course.

MR. HUGHES. Good Lord! Amy! *(Shakes head)* So she's starting now.

MIKE. *(Still facing TOMMY)* You and Jean ought to make a pair all right. Well, I hope you have a hot time at my party.

TOMMY. *Your* party?

(The DOORBELL rings.)

SNAZZY. Want me to go, Mr. Hughes?

MR. HUGHES. I wish you would, son. Your father's getting fallen arches from answering doorbells.

(SNAZZY crosses to Right and disappears.)

TOMMY. *(To MIKE—belligerently)* What are you doing here anyway?

MIKE. Wouldn't you like to know, Steinie?

(SNAZZY ushes CHARLES COLLIER into the room. He is tall and rather thin, with a good deal too much dignity for his age—twenty years. He speaks precisely and has an annoying way of cocking an eyebrow. He wears evening clothes and carries a very large corsage box.)

SNAZZY. Mr. Hughes, this is Charles Collier. *(Remains near hall door.)*

CHARLES. *(Crossing to Center)* How do you do, Mr. Hughes?

MR. HUGHES. *(Rising and extending his hand)* How do you do? Mildred will be down in a moment. Make yourself comfortable.

(They shake hands.)

TOMMY. *(To MIKE, who is still facing him)* And stop calling me "Steinie." It makes me mad.

MIKE. *(To the OTHERS)* And when Steinie gets mad, you should see him foam at the mouth. *(Sees CHARLES)* —How-ya, Collier? *(Takes a few steps toward Center.)*

CHARLES. Hello, Tisdale. *(Sits at Right end of sofa.)*

TOMMY. *(Crossing to stand close behind MIKE)*. One of these days, Mike, you're going to go too far—

MIKE. *(Turning)* Relax, Steinie—or I'll have Snazzy pin your ears back for you.

MR. HUGHES. You know, boys, I've got three daughters. I listen to them talk all the time. I've often wondered how boys talked when they got together. And now I know—they talk just like girls. *(To CHARLES)* —I understand you're going into banking one of these days.

CHARLES. As soon as I finish college. I'm going to be Vice-President. *(Cautiously)* But I'm not serious about girls. I just go with a lot of different ones.

MR. HUGHES. *(Concealing a smile)* I was just making conversation, Mr. Collier—not sizing you up for a son-in-law.

CHARLES. Well, you know how it is, Mr. Hughes. A fellow in my position has to be rather—cautious.

MR. HUGHES. I understand. *(Distastefully)* I can just see the women pursuing you down the street.

CHARLES. *(Stiffening)* Well, I didn't mean—

AMY. *(Appears on stairs. She is handsomely gowned but a trifle on the awkward side nevertheless. She comes down very fast and goes directly to SNAZZY at Right)* Good evening, Snazzy.

SNAZZY. Gee, Amy—gee, you look swell. Well, what do you know?

AMY. Didn't you expect me to look swell?

SNAZZY. Yeh—but not that swell. Gee!

MIKE. *(Shrugging)* Some line, huh?

SNAZZY. Amy—you know what I forgot? Flowers. I didn't even *think* of flowers. I knew I was forgetting something all evening.

AMY. I don't mind, Snazzy. *(Takes his hand.)*

(MILDRED appears on stairs, descends regally. CHARLES rises, as does MR. HUGHES. CHARLES crosses to meet MILDRED at foot of stairs. Bows slightly. MILDRED smiles at him. He offers the flower box.)

MILDRED. Thank you, Charles.

CHARLES. *(Walking to down Left with MILDRED, who is opening box, dropping ribbons and tissue over sofa)* It isn't much. Just an orchid.

MILDRED. *(Thrilled)* An orchid!

(They are now down Left and he pins orchid to her gown during following.)

MIKE. *(To MR. HUGHES)* Mr. H, ole man, you got a good-looking family. Yessir, a couple of pips if I ever saw 'em.

TOMMY. What's the matter with Jean?

MIKE. Oh, Jean's okay. She's fine. She's just your type, Steinie. She doesn't have to be good-looking.

TOMMY. She's good-looking enough for me.

MR. HUGHES. *(Starting up Center toward French windows)* I think I'll get some air.

(But before he gets out JEAN appears on stairs. JEAN wears a very attractive gown; her hair is loose and shining, beautifully coiffured; she has dispensed with her glasses. In all, she resembles the girl in Act One only remotely. Her eyes are shining. She pauses on stairs. MR. HUGHES sees her first.)

MR. HUGHES. *(Surprised)* Jean!

(The OTHERS turn and watch JEAN take a few more steps. Her eyes sweep the room.)

SNAZZY. *(Softly)* Wow!

AMY. *(Not so softly)* Jean! What have you done to yourself?

CHARLES. *(Approvingly)* Well—!

MIKE. *(Recovering and crossing to stairs)* Jean! Is this Jean? *(Rubs eyes exaggeratedly)* I can't believe my eyes! *(Makes a bow to her, half-mocking, but obviously he is attracted)* Enter, Queen.

(TOMMY has remained silent a little Right of Center.)

JEAN. *(To the room)* Good evening. Everyone ready? *(Even her voice has a fresh, intriguing vibrancy.)*

MIKE. Ready, willing and able, Queen.

(He reaches his hand toward her, but JEAN, as though. she doesn't see him, goes by him, ignoring his hand, and goes to TOMMY and slips her arm through his.)

TOMMY. What's all the fuss about, anyway?

JEAN. I want to thank you for the carnations, Tommy. They're lovely. *(Fingers them lightly.)*

TOMMY. You're welcome.—The way everybody's acting, you'd think you'd changed or something.

MIKE. *(Coming down to Left of JEAN)* You could at least speak to a fella, Princess.

JEAN. *(As though seeing him for first time)* Oh, hello, Mike. I didn't see you.

MIKE. Didn't see—! What is this?

(MR. HUGHES comes down to behind sofa.)

SNAZZY. Mike, you're gonna be late getting Ruth— and you know how sore she gets.

MIKE. *(Intrigued, angered, bewildered)* What time is it? I can't go now. *(To JEAN)* What do you mean— you didn't see me? What's the gag? *(With vast approval)* Say, you look keen! You're a gee-eyeful if I ever saw one! *(Looks at watch)* Holy Mackeral, it *is* late!

JEAN. *(Tantalizingly)* Better hurry, Mike. You know how sore Ruth gets.

MIKE. But I don't want to go now— I can't— *(Fas-*

tening his wrath on TOMMY) —You can't go with this bookworm!

JEAN. Of course I can, Mike. *(Smiles bewitchingly)* I'll see you later—at the party.

MIKE. *(Shifting from one foot to other)* Well—can I have a dance? Several dances? I mean—

JEAN. *(Simultaneously with* TOMMY'S *next line)* We'll see.

TOMMY. *(At same time—positively)* No!!

MIKE. Well, I gotta run. Save me a couple, Princess —maybe five. *(Crosses to hall at Right, while still looking at* JEAN) Sorry—I gotta go, sorry— *(Disappears. DOOR slams.)*

AMY. *(Clapping* JEAN *on back—hard)* Routed! You routed him! He's retreating! What a sister! *(Returns to* SNAZZY) Let's go, Snazzy. Ain't she a whizz? *(Takes* SNAZZY'S *arm and they exit Right.)*

CHARLES. *(To* MILDRED) Shall we go, Mildred?

MILDRED. I'd love to, Charles.

(They cross to Right during following.)

CHARLES. *(To* MR. HUGHES) I'm happy to have met you, Mr. Hughes. I'm taking your daughter to the Riviera Club. My father's a member, of course.

MILDRED. *(Kissing* MR. HUGHES *on cheek)* Goodnight, Daddy.

MR. HUGHES. Goodnight, Mildred.

(CHARLES and MILDRED continue to Right and exit.)

JEAN. *(To* TOMMY) Would you mind waiting on the porch half a minute, Tommy?   *(WARN Curtain.)*

TOMMY. Okay. *(To* MR. HUGHES) Goodnight, sir.

MR. HUGHES. Goodnight, Tommy.

(TOMMY, with a last look at JEAN, *goes out Right. A pause.* JEAN *turns to look at her father. He smiles and crosses slowly toward her at Center.)*

JEAN. *(Softly)* Well, Daddy—you haven't said how you like me.

MR. HUGHES. *(Also softly)* I'm like Tommy—I always knew you were beautiful.

JEAN. Thank you, Daddy.

MR. HUGHES. But where did you learn all this stuff? You twisted Mike into a little ball and rolled him out the door—do you know that?

JEAN. *(With a smile)* I told you I was going to be the life of the party from now on, didn't I? *(She straightens his tie)* I told you to watch my dust, didn't I?

MR. HUGHES. You be careful of that dust, Daughter. It's star-dust you're throwing around. You're liable to get hurt. But I am glad you've decided to stick to Tommy—not that other inflated balloon.

JEAN. Mike is *not*, Daddy. And I haven't decided on Tommy at all. Don't be so naive. *(Walks up to look out French windows—slowly)* I *like* Tommy—but— *(Very quietly)* I think I *love* Mike. *(Leans in window.)*

MR. HUGHES. *(Sinking to sofa—quietly)* No— No— Anything but that.

JEAN. *(Immediately spirited again, returns to MR. HUGHES)* Don't be an old fogie, Daddy. *(Kisses him lightly)* You'll like Mike when you get to know him. *(Starts for hall Right—happily)* I've never felt so good in my whole life before!

(JEAN disappears. MR. HUGHES is shaking his head.)

MR. HUGHES. *(Mumbling)* Anything but that—anything but that— *(Disgustedly)* "Mr. H—ole man!" *(Stretches out on sofa)* Lord, I'm glad I'm an old man.

(The Curtain drops briefly to denote the passing of about three hours. When it rises again the party is in full swing. The room has been disarranged: the furniture at crazy angles, coke bottles everywhere, etc. At the moment there is no one on stage but radio MUSIC can be heard from the garden. Behind the French windows vari-colored Chinese lanterns can be seen. Occasionally a guest or two passes by the windows, which are open. Through-

out the following, the MUSIC can be heard softly in the background. Whenever the French windows open, we hear the VOICES; they increase in intensity as the Act progresses. After a moment in which the voices mingle with the music, TEDDY *and* HOPE SHUTTLEWORTH, *the gushing pretty girl from Act One, enter from Right. She is in a complaining mood and* TEDDY *is trying to placate her.)*

TEDDY. Now don't get whipped up, Hope. I couldn't help it.

HOPE. But Teddy, I stood there in the hall at school —waiting and waiting for you—and everybody else went home—and still I stood there—then the janitor turned out the lights. I felt like a fool. Where *were* you?

TEDDY. I told you: I thought of something I forgot to do—I had to go do it.

HOPE. *(Sitting on sofa)* Frankly, Teddy—I don't understand you. You haven't treated me the way I ought to be treated all evening. *(Pouting)* You only danced every third dance with me—*all evening!*

TEDDY. I know, Hope. You see— *(At Right end of sofa)* Well, it's this way—I get confused when I dance. All that turning and turning and kicking. The blood goes to my head—

(DOTTIE KIXMILLER *enters quickly through French windows and comes down to Right of* TEDDY.)

DOTTIE. *(As she enters, in her gruff voice)* There you are, Hughes. What is this—the runaround? I can't sit out there by myself all night— *(Sees* HOPE) Oh!

HOPE. *(Rising)* Hello, Dottie.

DOTTIE. Hello, Hope. *(Belligerently to* TEDDY) Did I interrupt something?

TEDDY. *(Worried)* Not at all. Glad to see you, Dottie.

HOPE. *(To* DOTTIE) You seem to be chasing Teddy something awful, Dottie. Every time I turned around this evening at the Prom, you were dancing with him.

DOTTIE. Yeah? And you want to know something

funny? Every time I turned around, he was dancing with you! What do you think of that?

TEDDY. *(In between—and mopping his brow)* Now, girls, let's not get—

HOPE. *(Sweetly)* Why shouldn't he dance with me? I can't help it if he seems to like me, can I?

DOTTIE. *(Arms akimbo)* You're the helpless type. You can't help *anything!*

TEDDY. *(Quickly, blithely)* That's right. None of us can help anything.—May I get you something— *(Quickly)* either of you? Some punch? *Some*thing? *Any*thing?

HOPE. No, thanks, dear.

DOTTIE. Don't bother, Hughes. *(To* HOPE*)* Where do you get that "dear" stuff anyway, Shuttleworth?

(The TELEPHONE rings.)

TEDDY. Shhhhh—! *(Holds up a finger. The TELE-PHONE rings again. He smiles)* I thought I heard it. *(Crosses to desk.)*

DOTTIE. *(To* HOPE*)* You're just the type that'd call any boy "dear." *(Flings herself into Right Center chair.)*

TEDDY. Shhhh. *(Picks up telephone)* Hughes residence— Oh, yes, sir. Yes, sir. *(To room)* It's a neighbor.—I know it's loud, but that's Tommy Dorsey, sir. Don't you *like* Tommy Dorsey?—That's funny. Most people do—I'll see what I can do— Maybe you'd like Harry James better— *(Shudders and holds telephone away from ear; grimaces)* All right, sir. I'll tell them to turn it down. *(Laughs artificially)* But you know the younger generation— No, it's not very late, sir— you must be an early riser. It's not quite midnight— Goodbye—and you be careful. I'll bet your face is purple. *(Replaces telephone; mops his brow)* Whew! That was Mr. Matson. He lives next door and he doesn't like either Tommy Dorsey or Harry James.— He must be kind of batty.

DOTTIE. *(Stalking up to* TEDDY *at desk)* Listen, Hughes—there's something darned funny around here—

TEDDY. *(Quickly assuming control)* Come on, Hope. *(Takes* DOTTIE'S *arm while* HOPE *rises)* Come on, Dottie. We gotta quiet down that racket before Mr. Matson gets really tough. His blood pressure's rising. *(*HOPE *has come to him; he takes her arm)* Come on. *(Turns to French windows)* Mingle with the crowd, girls. Tell them to smother the gabble. *(One girl on each arm, he hurries out, pushing them a bit.)*

(There is a pause. If anything, the MUSIC grows louder and now that no one is on stage, we hear the clatter of VOICES—the squeals of the GIRLS, *the harsh laughter of the* BOYS—*more distinctly. Then* TOMMY, *looking pretty dejected, comes in and closes the French windows after him. He wanders down to table, picks up a magazine, scans it as he walks around Left end of sofa, sinks to sofa, tosses magazine to other end in a quick angry movement; leans forward, his head in his hands.—Then the French windows open again and* JEAN, *looking even more radiant and excited, enters and starts, humming, to Left door. Just as she reaches it and starts to exit,* TOMMY *speaks—)*

TOMMY. Happy?

JEAN. *(Turning)* Oh—hello, Tommy. Yes, I'm happy. *(Steps toward him)* What's the matter with you?

TOMMY. I'm a sour puss—from way back.

JEAN. What are you doing in here, anyway?

TOMMY. Reading a magazine. *(Points to magazine)* I just learned how to lose ten pounds without dieting. —Jean, aren't you just a little worried about all this?

JEAN. Worried? No—why?

TOMMY. *(Rising)* About how all this will turn out. —Do you *like* that gang out there?

JEAN. Most of them—yes. Very much. I'm sorry you don't care for my friends, Tommy King.

TOMMY. They're not your friends. You hardly know them, Jean. *(Takes her wrist)* Listen, you want some good advice—? Get rid of that crowd before it gets any wilder.

JEAN. *(Softly)* Tommy, you're holding my hand.

TOMMY. *(Dropping her wrist)* I am not!

JEAN. I didn't say I minded.

TOMMY. Jean, you confuse me. One minute you act like Mike Tisdale is the only fellow you ever saw with your eyes open—and the next minute you tell me to hold your hand.

JEAN. *(From lofty heights)* My dear boy, I haven't told you to hold my hand. I don't need to ask people to hold my hand. Most boys want to—tonight. *(With this final pronouncement, she turns and steps toward Left door)* Pardon me while I get more potato chips. *(Exits.)*

(TOMMY looks after her, shakes his head, flops himself back onto sofa, reaches for magazine again. He opens it, starts to read; his anger gets the better of him and he stands up and hurls the magazine to the Right, all the way across room. Just at this moment AMY enters through French windows; she also looks depressed.)

AMY. *(Pausing up)* Hey, what's the idea?

TOMMY. *(Grouchily)* What's it to you?

AMY. *(Coming down Center)* What's the matter, Tommy? Is that sister of mine stepping all over you?

TOMMY. *(Crosses and sits in down Right chair)* No. —Oh, I don't know.

AMY. *(Sitting in Right Center chair)* I know what's the matter with you: you're in love. Isn't it awful?

TOMMY. I never felt this way before—and I don't like it.

AMY. That's love.—I got the same trouble.

TOMMY. What's the matter with her—that's what I want to know? In Physics class she seemed like she had some sense. She understood things. But tonight— *(Shakes head.)*

AMY. It's that Mike fellow. She's under his charm. He's a he-witch.

TOMMY. *(Standing up suddenly)* Well, if she likes a fellow like that, she's not the girl for me! *(Starts to*

63

Right door) I'm going home. *(Pauses at door)* —Darn it, I can't go home! *(He crosses behind the Right Center chair and sits on Right arm of sofa)* See—I'm caught.

AMY. You're caught, bound, tied and gagged. Brother, I pity you. *(Leans forward with head in hands—dejected)* —I wish I was dead myself.

TOMMY. *(Interested)* You do? What's the matter with *you?*

AMY. That Snazzy does anything Mike tells him.

TOMMY. *(Bitterly)* Doesn't everyone?

AMY. *I* don't.

TOMMY. Jean does. *(Sinks into sofa; slouches.)*

AMY. *(Sadly)* Yeh. How can I fall for a fella like that? Weak-kneed, hopeless, sappy— (SNAZZY, *as described, enters through French windows, and comes tentatively down to Center)* —flea-brained, no grit, no will of his own, just a shadow.

SNAZZY. *(In a voice that breaks)* Hello, Amy.

AMY. Hello, hopeless.

SNAZZY. Am I interrupting something?

AMY. Just your own obituary.

SNAZZY. What have I done now, Amy?

AMY. Everything. Go away.

SNAZZY. All right, Amy. If that's the way you feel. Okay. *(Starts sadly for French windows again, then thinks of something; turns)* —Does your father have any golf clubs handy, Amy?

AMY. In the closet. Why?

SNAZZY. *(Going to closet up Left, opening door)* Well, you know Mike's sister Muriel. She's a golf fiend. Wants to practise, I guess. Mike said to get her some clubs. *(Goes into closet.)*

AMY. "Mike said!" *(Rises)* You follow orders like Arthur Treacher!

SNAZZY. *(Emerging from closet with bag of golf clubs)* What did you say, Amy?

AMY. *(Taking a threatening step toward him)* I said I ought to wrap a putter around your neck!

SNAZZY. *(Breaking and running with golf-bag*

toward French windows and out) I can't see what's come over everyone. *(He is gone.)*

AMY. *(Turning to* TOMMY*)* What can she do with golf clubs at midnight? Even Mike's sister ought to have more sense. *(Goes to behind sofa; places hand on* TOMMY's *shoulder)* —Tommy, I guess this is what the books refer to as "first love." Afterwards, they say you're older and wiser— *(Harshly)* But what if you murder someone in between?

TOMMY. Then you don't get older.

AMY. I think I'll go practise a cheer. *(Exits up Center.)*

JEAN. *(Enters from Left, carrying a huge bowl of potato chips—as huge a bowl as it is possible to obtain, perhaps a large salad bowl. She pauses at Left end of sofa. Reproachfully)* Tommy, are you still moping around?

TOMMY. *(Rising, goes to stand close to* JEAN*)* No, I'm not moping. I'm thinking. I'm thinking hard. Just because you've let your hair down, you don't have to start acting like those numbskull friends of Mike's.

JEAN. Tommy, I really think you're becoming jealous. *(Sets potato chips on down Left chair)* And you shouldn't, really. *(Her voice is becoming more and more liquid)* Because I *am* fond of you, Tommy— *(Takes his lapels in her hands)* and I did have such a good time at the Prom—

TOMMY. *(Weakening)* Yes, you did—dancing every other dance with Mike Tisdale.

JEAN. But Tommy—you know how it is if a girl dances every dance with her date. People will think we're going together—and—

TOMMY. Let them think it! I'd like to go with you. *(Places his arms around her.)*

JEAN. You may—but not all the time, Tommy. *(Staring into his eyes in a particularly bewitching manner)* And I'm glad because you're jealous, but at the same time I wish you wouldn't be—in a way—though of course it does make me feel good to know that you care enough—more about me than those Physics experiments, I mean—

TOMMY. *(Leaning toward her, as though to kiss)* Jean—Jean— You're driving me as crazy as all the other kids around here.

JEAN. *(Ready to kiss him)* Maybe that's good for you, Tommy.

(Just as the kiss is about to be completed, the French windows open and RUTH COATES enters. She also wears an evening gown, of course.)

RUTH. Very interesting. *(Hands on hips)* Very intresting indeed!

(JEAN and TOMMY break apart. TOMMY walks nervously to Right.)

JEAN. *(Pleasantly—pleased with herself)* Isn't it, Ruth?

RUTH. You're certainly mowing them down, Jean— one, two, three. *(Coming to Center)* I wish *I'd* thought of that gag of wearing glasses and pinning my hair up for a couple of weeks.

JEAN. *(Turning to pick up potato chips)* Try it some time. It's really fun.

MIKE. *(Enters through French windows. He is as brash and enthusiastic as ever)* What's everybody doing in here? The party's out there.—And some party, eh? *(Goes to Center)* You ever hear of that Truth and Consequences game? Well, how's this—I got a new angle on it. You don't tell the truth about yourself— you tell the truth about your date! Say, that oughta be a riot!

RUTH. It ought to *cause* a riot—at least. *(Sits on arm of Right Center chair.)*

MIKE. Aw, you're a kill-joy. *(Steps toward JEAN)* —What do you say, Jean? Sure, Jean'll like it.

JEAN. You mean someone asks me questions and I have to tell the truth about Tommy?

MIKE. *(Going to her)* Sure. Like I'd ask: "Did Tommy try to kiss you on the way to the Prom?" And you'd have to tell the truth and tell what both of you said.—Pretty good, eh?

RUTH. Let's play right now, Mike. Suppose I ask you: "Which girl is your date tonight—Ruth Coates or Jean Hughes?" What would you say?

MIKE. (*Stepping toward* RUTH—*knows he's on the spot*) Aw now, Ruth—

RUTH. (*Unmoved—levelly*) Which is your date—and why don't you act like it?

MIKE. Say, we haven't started yet.

TOMMY. (*Crosses swiftly, determinedly to* JEAN) And I might ask the same question!

JEAN. (*Taken back*) Tommy, I—

MIKE. (*Coming up behind* TOMMY) Say, Steinie—don't start getting tough with girls now. (*Takes* TOMMY'S *arm and swings him around*) I don't like to hear you talking like that to a lady.

TOMMY. Let go my arm.

MIKE. What if I don't want to, Steinie?

RUTH. (*Stepping in—to Right of* MIKE) You think you're pretty tough, Mike, just because you played football. Why don't you pick on someone your own size?

TOMMY. Thank you, Ruth.

JEAN. Tommy, I wouldn't let anyone talk to me that way—no matter what size he is.

TOMMY. (*Shakes his head and goes to sit on chair down Left*) Jean, I'm disappointed in you. Don't you know by now—I'm no man of action. I *think* my way out of things. I have to give this a good think.

RUTH. You're right, Tommy. Mike's just a bully.

JEAN. (*To* RUTH—*hotly*) Mike is *not* a bully! You're angry because you're losing him.

MIKE. Now girls, maybe Tommy's right after all; we *haven't* been thinking much this evening.

RUTH. (*To* JEAN) If that's the way you feel about it, Jean—why don't we trade dates right here and now?

TOMMY. I'm certainly willing.

RUTH. I'm more than willing.

JEAN. It's all right with me.

MIKE. (*Very loud*) No—no—I'm not willing! *No!*

RUTH. (*With disgust as she goes Right*) Holy Harry

67

ACT II

—*men!* You never know **which** way they're going to turn!

JEAN. *(Stepping toward* MIKE—*angry)* So you don't want a date with me—after all!

MIKE. *(Trying to play both ends)* Jean, I didn't say that. I mean: I want to do the right thing. I want to do whatever's right—whatever that is.

JEAN. You mean you *don't* want a date with me—!

MIKE. Of course I do, Jean, only—

RUTH. *(Stepping in—also angry)* So you *do* want a date with her! Well, you can have it—starting right now! I think it's about time I started seeing more of other boys anyway. Don't forget I was once voted the most popular girl in our class!

MIKE. Ruth, I know that. Listen to me—I know that! Holy Mackerel! Don't let something like this separate us!

RUTH. Mr. Tisdale, we're already separated—as of now!

MIKE. Ruth, you can't—

JEAN. I'm glad to know this is how you *really* feel, Mike Tisdale!

MIKE. *(From one to other)* Now, Jean—now, Ruth —*(Lost)*—aw, what's the matter here, anyway?

TOMMY. *(Standing up suddenly)* Tisdale, I think you're treating Ruth pretty shabbily.

(A pause.)

JEAN. *(Recovering)* Tommy! I think you really *do* want to go with Ruth.

TOMMY. *(Reasonably)* Why shouldn't I? You want to go with Mike.

JEAN. But that's different— *(Sits on sofa)* —I'm lost. My head's going around. *(To* TOMMY*)* What side are you on, anyway? (ALL *are watching her)* Love baffles me. I almost wish I were back where I started —ugly and unpopular.

RUTH. You don't seem to be so popular *now*, do you?

TOMMY. Popularity! Is that all girls think of? *(To* JEAN*)* —I thought you had more sense! I'm disgusted with the whole lot of you!

MIKE. *(Stepping closer)* All right, wise guy! I told you not to talk that way to Jean. Stop it!

RUTH. *(To MIKE)* "To Jean!" "To *Jean!*" What do you care how he talks to Jean?

TOMMY. *(As excited as he has ever been in his life)* *Leaping atoms!* Here we go again! I'm getting out of here before I go completely nuts! *(Rushes Center, fast, going in several directions)* Where's my hat? I'm going— *(During this* MR. HUGHES *comes down the stairs, pauses on stairs and watches* TOMMY's *frenzy.)* Oh, I didn't have a hat. All right—goodbye! This is the craziest night of my life! This place is like a merry-go-round that got out of control! *(Making circles in the air)* Round and round ninety miles an hour! *(More circles)* Round and round! *(Stands helplessly in middle of room)* I'm so mixed up and mad I could *(With a growl)* tear the house down!

MR. HUGHES. Tommy, what's the matter? I thought you were different from the others. *(Comes down stairs)* I thought you had some intelligence.

TOMMY. *(Going madly to* MR. HUGHES*)* I did have some intelligence when I came in here! It's all gone now! *A man can stand just so much!*

MR. HUGHES. Tommy, you're going to burst a blood vessel.

TOMMY. *I WANT to burst a blood vessel! (Turns to* OTHERS*)* And just don't forget, any of you—there are more important things than brawn. I'll win yet! Remember that! Wise men always win because they attack the *mind*— *(Crosses to face* MIKE *at one inch range)* of their opponent! They win because they attack mentally and *(His voice trembling)* because they keep their heads! *They keep their heads! (He dashes out through French windows.)*

(A pause.)

MR. HUGHES. What have you been doing to that boy?

RUTH. That's the scientific mind at work.

MR. HUGHES. *(There is a CRASH outside—as of*

glass smashing—but at a distance. MR. HUGHES, *looking startled, goes quickly to French windows)* Now what? *(Goes.)*

JEAN. Maybe Tommy tried to cool himself off in the punch bowl.

(The DOORBELL rings. JEAN *crosses to Right and goes into hall.)*

RUTH. I hope you're satisfied with yourself, Mike. *(Crosses down Left.)*

MIKE. *(Following)* Ruth, you've got to listen to me a minute. I know it looks funny to you, but you've got to understand me—

RUTH. *(Facing him—quietly angry)* I'm afraid that's my weakness: I understand you.

MIKE. *(Throwing himself into sofa)* Well, what the devil am I supposed to do?

*(*JEAN *returns; with her is* SALLY FRAZIER, *a pleasant girl,* TEDDY'S *age.* SALLY *is dressed for traveling and carries a bag. She is given to easy tears, as we shall see.* JEAN *pauses Center.* SALLY *is speaking as they enter.)*

SALLY. I didn't recognize you at first, Jean. I didn't mean to break in on a party or anything.

JEAN. *(Introducing)* Sally, this is Ruth Coates— And this is Mike Tisdale.—Sally Frazier from Sheridan City.

*(*RUTH *and* MIKE *greet her,* MIKE *standing up.)*

SALLY. How do you do? *(To* JEAN*)* —Teddy kept writing, asking me to come any time I wanted to. He said you had plenty of room, so I—

JEAN. Teddy'll be delighted to see you. Sit down, Sally.

SALLY. Thanks, Jean. I can't wait to see Teddy's face. *(Sits in Right Center chair.)*

JEAN. *(With irony)* Neither can I.

*(Outside, SINGING accompanies the RADIO now;
many voices raised pretty high in chorus. SALLY
gets up and goes swiftly to the French windows;
looks out.)*

SALLY. I just *love* parties! *(JEAN sits on sofa next
to MIKE. RUTH sits down Left. All three are glumly
staring ahead)* It sounds like so much fun.
JEAN. *(Unenthusiastically)* Yeah.
RUTH. *(The same way)* Yeah.
MIKE. *(Very sour)* Un-huh.
SALLY. *(Getting excited)* Ohhh! Here comes Teddy.
(Then louder) With a girl—with *another girl!* (Steps
to Left of French windows; sinks unobtrusively to the
hassock.)*

*(The French windows open, letting in a particularly
loud BLAST of noise: the music, the singing, and
perhaps in the background five or six people prac-
tising a school cheer—undoubtedly under AMY'S
direction. TEDDY enters with MARYROSALIE VOGUL-
HUT, she of the deep silences. TEDDY is talking.)*

TEDDY. That's the thing you girls have to understand. A fella like me—we do things a little differently.
(To the room, as he leads MARYROSALIE down Right)
—Hi-ya, everybody. *(To MARYROSALIE)* —We don't
limit ourselves, you might say—like ordinary fellows.
I can tell by the way you're acting you're jealous. *Are
you? (No answer)* Are you, Maryrosalie? *(MARYRO-
SALIE looks him in the eye, her lips compress, and she
stomps one foot; without a word, she turns and goes
into the garden again; closes the French windows after
her. Sitting in Right chair)* Funny girl, that Maryrosalie. Never says a word but you always know what she's
thinking. Pretty, though, isn't she? *(Sees the long
faces)* —What's the matter in here? You look like
three stiffs in a morgue.
JEAN. Thanks.
RUTH. Thank you, sir.
MIKE. Aw, shut up.

TEDDY. Okay—I don't mind resting in here a moment. A party like this wears me out—all those girls.

(SALLY *remains silent upstage.* HOPE SHUTTLEWORTH *enters up Center, closes windows, goes directly to* TEDDY.)

HOPE. Oh, here you are, Teddy. You're the oddest boy—I can never find you. And here you are sitting in here by your little lonesome self. *(Sits on arm of his chair.)*
TEDDY. *(Putting an arm around her)* You mean you're not sore any more, Hope?
HOPE. *(Running a hand through his hair)* I won't be sore any more—ever—if you'll always be like this—
SALLY. *(Rises and crosses to Center; she faces* TEDDY, *who hasn't seen her)* Teddy Hughes—*who is this woman?!*

(HOPE *leaps up.* TEDDY *looks bewildered and caught.* SALLY, *hands on hips, faces them.)*

MIKE. *(Quietly)* Aw, shut up.
HOPE. *(To* TEDDY) Who's this now?
SALLY. Teddy—*who is this woman?!*
TEDDY. *(Rising)* Oh—oh, hi-ya, Sally? What you doing here? I mean—when'd you get here? I mean—how long you been here?
SALLY. Long *enough*, Teddy Hughes. You wrote me to come. You *begged* me. Your letters *dripped!*
HOPE. Letters! *(To* TEDDY) Do you write her letters too?
SALLY. He started writing me letters when we were in kindergarten together.
TEDDY. *(Deciding to have it out)* Well, Sally—haven't you been having—I mean—I can't imagine you sitting home by yourself—I mean—you probably have other dates.
SALLY. *(Loud)* Of course I have—but you *promised me!* I didn't promise *you!*

(AMY *and* SNAZZY *enter up Center.* AMY *wears a wor-*

ried look. SNAZZY *looks determined. He marches down to* MIKE.)

SNAZZY. Mike—
MIKE. Go away. I'm busy.
HOPE. Teddy, you're the most fickle, deceitful man I've ever known!
AMY. *(Beside* SNAZZY *and urging him on)* Go on, Snazzy—tell him!
SNAZZY. *(To* MIKE—*in earnest)* Mike, Amy thinks —that is, *I* think—*we* think—we ought to call the party off. Tell everyone to go home.

(TELEPHONE rings. TEDDY, *eager to get away from the* GIRLS, *dashes up to answer it.)*

MIKE. Go away.
SNAZZY. But listen—
TEDDY. *(Picking up telephone)* Quiet, everybody! *(Into telephone)* Hughes residence— Yes, Mr. Matson— Yes, Mr. Matson.
SALLY. *(Unable to restrain herself, follows* TEDDY*)* And I'm going home right now—back to Sheridan City—tonight—if I have to *hitch-hike!* *(Bursts into tears.)*
TEDDY. *(Holding hand over telephone—in loud whisper)* Sally, you can't do that! Now wait a min— *(Into phone)* Wait a minute, Mr. Matson. *(To* SALLY*)* Sit down and let's talk it— *(Into telephone)* I said: *wait a minute!*
SALLY. *(Weeping now)* Where's my suitcase? I should have stayed in Sheridan City—where everything's quiet. *(Picks up bag and starts for Right.)*
TEDDY. *(Into telephone)* I'll talk to you later. Goodbye. *(Hangs up and starts after* SALLY*)* —Now, Sally, you just got the wrong impression, coming in like that—
SALLY. *(Faces him near Right door, her face tearstained)* Teddy Hughes, I could murder you!
AMY. *(To* SNAZZY*)* Well, are you going to tell him or aren't you?

(TEDDY *and* SALLY *continue their argument in quiet tones but with many gestures during following.*)

SNAZZY. Mike—the party's getting out of hand. That was the neighbors complaining. Amy says we gotta go home, all of us.

MIKE. (*Standing up*) Who do you think you're talking to, Snazz?

SNAZZY. (*Facing him—in a little voice*) I'm telling you—I think.

MIKE. (*Taking* SNAZZY *by shirt front or necktie*) Well, I'm telling *you!* I've got enough trouble and you better get back out there and leave me alone.

SNAZZY. (*Bullied*) Okay, Mike, okay. Let go. Okay.

AMY. (*Stepping in*) You bully! (*She smacks* MIKE *across the face—hard.*)

(MIKE *lets go of* SNAZZY. *All are startled.* RUTH *and* JEAN *rise.* TEDDY *and* SALLY *turn, pause. There are general exclamations.*)

MIKE. (*Angry, starts for* AMY, *who dashes upstage*) Say, girl or no girl, I'll—

(*As* MIKE *reaches Center,* TEDDY *steps toward him; blocks his way.*)

TEDDY. That's my sister, Tisdale.

(*There is a dramatic pause while* ALL *wait to see what will happen. Into it steps* MR. HUGHES *from garden; he carries his bag of golf-sticks.*)

MR. HUGHES. (*Seeing the fighting positions and the general anticipation*) Every time I walk into this room, I wish I hadn't. (*Steps to between* TEDDY *and* MIKE) I don't know what it's all about, but you two better quiet down. (*Displays golf bag*) Do you know what your friends were doing out there—driving my good golf balls down the alley—in the dark. They broke the Matsons' window—and Lord knows how many others.

(MIKE *and* TEDDY *drop their belligerent poses.*)

AMY. That's what I've been telling them! That's what I've been saying! They've got to go home!

MR. HUGHES. Is your mother home yet? Your mother ought to be here. *(To* AMY*)* Did you start them on those cheers out there? They've got the whole neighborhood awake.

AMY. I started them—but I can't stop them now.

MR. HUGHES. You better stop them. Get out there and stop them in two minutes or I'll do it myself!

SNAZZY. *(As* AMY *moves to French windows)* Want me to help, Amy?

AMY. You! You can't even help yourself. *(Tragically)* Isn't that life? The first man you fall in love with turns out to be a coward! *(Exits.)*

SNAZZY. *(Following)* Amy, wait for me—I'm no coward— *(Disappears.)*

RUTH. *(Rising)* Mr. Hughes, Mike suggested a very quiet game a while ago—something like Truth or Consequences. I'll try to get that started—it should be quiet enough.

MR. HUGHES. The best idea I've heard all evening.

RUTH. Providing I get first turn. Just think—I get to answer questions anyone wants to ask about dear little Mike!.

JEAN. And *I've* got some questions!

RUTH. Well, come on. *(Starts for up Center.)*

JEAN. *(Following* RUTH*)* Coming, Mike?

MIKE. No— Yes— I mean—I guess I'd better.

(JEAN *and* RUTH *offer their arms and* MIKE, *between them, takes their arms and goes out. He is mopping his brow.*)

MR. HUGHES. *(Moving to stairs)* I hope that helps. *(Starts up)* I think I better stow these away in a safe place—what's left of them. *(Goes up.)*

(TEDDY *starts for French windows—but* SALLY, *who has remained up Right, and* HOPE, *who has*

watched from down Right, step toward him imme-
diately and prevent his escape.)

SALLY. Where do you think you're going?

TEDDY. I just thought of someone—I mean something—in the garden—I have to—

HOPE. If you go out that door, I'll never speak to
you again.

SALLY. And I'll go back to Sheridan City and tell
everyone what kind of a person you've turned into.

TEDDY. *(Defeated—slouches back to Right Center
chair—a warning voice)* You're going to be sorry if I
don't get out there soon. *(Sits)* We're all going to be
sorry.

*(SALLY goes to Right chair and HOPE perches on Right
arm of sofa. They listen. The NOISE outside has
subsided somewhat.)*

HOPE. *(Hopefully)* I think it's quieter, don't you?

SALLY. I don't even care. *(In a wail)* And I used to
love parties! *(Consumed with self-pity, she collapses
into sobs.)*

HOPE. *(To TEDDY)* Does she cry all the time?

TEDDY. I guess so. *(Rises)* Listen—if I don't get out
there soon—it's not going to be so quiet in here.

*(But before he can make a move, the French windows
open with a bang and DOTTIE KIXMILLER, full of
anger, determination and bitterness, enters, crosses
as she speaks to Center between TEDDY and HOPE.)*

DOTTIE. I'm not in the habit of chasing men around,
Hughes. I don't like it! It's undignified.

SALLY. *(In a louder wail)* Another one! Another
one! Not one, but *twoooo—!*

HOPE. *(To DOTTIE)* Did Teddy have a date with you
tonight, Dottie?

DOTTIE. He certainly did. And I'm getting tired of
being— *(She gets it, stops, hand to forehead)* —Don't
tell me he had a date with you too!

SALLY. *(Crying)* And he's been writing me letters—*love* letters—begging me to come from Sheridan City for a week-end!

TEDDY. *(Feebly)* Not *this* week-end.

(The French windows open again. MARYROSALIE enters, joins the OTHERS, facing TEDDY, who by now has begun to draw back within himself. When he sees MARYROSALIE he sinks back into the chair, his hands over his ears, his arms across his eyes as though he expects blows.)

SALLY. Who's this?

DOTTIE. *(Suspicious)* Who you dating tonight, anyway, Maryrosalie?

HOPE. She won't talk.

MARYROSALIE. *(Speaking for first time—in a shrill, loud, angry voice—directly to TEDDY)* I'm leaving your party! I'm leaving this house! I was never so insulted in my whole life. You don't know how to treat a lady! I've got a notion to get my brother to wipe the floor up with you! I ought to do it myself—right now!

DOTTIE. You'll get a lot of help.

MARYROSALIE. Just because I don't talk a lot doesn't mean I don't have any *feelings!*—If you ever so much as mention my name again, Mr. Hughes, I'll have my brother tear you into little pieces. *(Goes to Right door; turns to face TEDDY again. TEDDY has lowered his arms and turned to follow her with his eyes. He flinches as she turns)* And my brother's a Golden Gloves champion! *(She goes out. The outside DOOR slams.)*

(A pause. Then:)

TEDDY. Sally, I—-

HOPE. *(Quickly)* Sally, shall we go upstairs and powder our noses?

SALLY. *(Rising)* I'd love to, Hope.

HOPE. Dottie, what about you?

TEDDY. *(Trying to break in)* Dottie, I—

DOTTIE. *(Ignoring TEDDY—to HOPE)* I'm with you.

77   ACT II

(SALLY crosses to Center; joins OTHERS. They go to stairs during:)

HOPE. I just love that hat, Sally. Where'd you get it?

TEDDY. *(Following a few steps)* Sally, you know how I feel—

SALLY. A little shop in Sheridan City. Direct from New York.

DOTTIE. I think it's the nuts.

HOPE. It's darling.

SALLY. I'm so glad you like it.

(They are going up stairs. TEDDY has followed to foot of stairs.)

TEDDY. Wait a second now— Holy Smoke, I—!

SALLY. *(As they disappear)* Your gowns are lovely, both of them——

TEDDY. I said—!

(But the GIRLS have gone. Defeated, TEDDY stands at foot of stairs, staring up, mumbling. MILDRED enters with CHARLES COLLIER from Right.)

MILDRED. I forgot about my sister's party, Charles. I hope you don't mind—a kids' party, you know.

TEDDY. *(Suffering from a terrible frustration, wants to hit something or someone; instead, he pounds his fists on the newel post, mumbling—)* I'll never talk to another woman if I live to be a hundred! *(Turns)* I'm gonna take up football and forget 'em all! *(Looks up and sees CHARLES and MILDRED staring at him. Harshly)* Well, what are you looking at?

MILDRED. Teddy, act your age. What's come over you?

TEDDY. Plenty— *(Crosses to slump in sofa)* Nothing— Go away.

MILDRED. *(To CHARLES)* Growing pains, I guess.— Let's see what kind of a snack we can whip together in the kitchen.

CHARLES. *(Crossing to Left with MILDRED but look-*

ing uneasily, cocking an eyebrow, at TEDDY) I'd like to, very much.

MILDRED. Aren't children amusing at that age? *(Exits Left with* CHARLES.*)*

TEDDY. *(Lifelessly—with heavy irony)* Very amusing. Ha-ha.

MR. HUGHES. *(Comes down the stairs; seeing* TEDDY, *speaks)* I can't stay up there. With three girls talking and squealing and giggling in the next room.

TEDDY. *(Bitterly)* They can *giggle!*

(As MR. HUGHES *reaches foot of stairs,* JEAN *enters from up Center.)*

MR. HUGHES. Hello, life of the party. Having a good time?

JEAN. Don't tease, Daddy. I'm worried. *(Meets* MR. HUGHES *at Center)* They're playing that game and it's awful. Mugsy Fletcher is standing up spouting like Cicero, telling all the faults of his girl—and she's getting so mad she might do anything. No one can stop him.

MR. HUGHES. Maybe I better—do you think I could stop it?

JEAN. Maybe you'd better try. Clarissa—that's Mugsy's girl—is getting so mad she's liable to throw a birdbath at Mugsy any minute.

MR. HUGHES. Well, I never did anything like this before. *(Hunches shoulders bravely)* I'll—what'll I say?

JEAN. *(Urging him)* Go on. You can do it. Just imagine you're the President or somebody.

MR. HUGHES. Well, here goes. *(He throws open the French windows, goes just outside them, remains in sight. Raises his voice)* Say—everybody—attention— listen to me— *(The NOISE subsides)* Now we've all had a good time tonight—I think—and all I have to say is: I'm glad. *(CHEERS from outside—many voices.* MR. HUGHES *holds up his hand; gets silence)* And Jean is glad, too. *(More CHEERS, with a mingling of "Hurray for Jean! Good ole Jean! For she's a jolly good fellow!" etc. Again he holds up his hand; silence)* But I think you should all fold up your little tents and silently steal away. *(More shouts: "Isn't he a scream! Louder and funnier! For he's a jolly good fellow! Hurrah for Mr. Hughes!" etc.* MR. HUGHES *turns to* JEAN —*in a low voice)* They think I'm kidding. *(To the crowd—very loud)* I'm not kidding! I think you should all go home now. *(More CHEERS.)*

JEAN. It's no use, Daddy.

MR. HUGHES. *(To the crowd—a last attempt)* You're too loud and it's getting late—and I'm getting tired— *(Even louder CHEERS.* MR. HUGHES *shakes his head, returns to room, closes windows)* Do you think they'd get the idea if I wandered among them with a baseball bat?

JEAN. *(Going to sit in Right Center chair)* I doubt it.—It's all my fault.

MR. HUGHES. Now don't start taking all the blame, Jean.—Let me have some of it.

(He starts to sit on Right arm of sofa, but leaps up at the tremendous CRASH from the garden—breaking glass, smashing fender, etc. Then feminine screams.)

MR. HUGHES. What the—!

JEAN. *(Rising)* Somebody's car—!

TEDDY. *(Also rising—wildly) My* car! That's my car out there—with the radio going! *(Dashing wildly for French windows.)*

(AMY and SNAZZY enter, out of breath, at up Center, stopping TEDDY.)

AMY. *(Barring the door)* I don't think I'd go out there, Teddy.

TEDDY. Out of my way!

AMY. Not if I were you—I wouldn't go out there!

MR. HUGHES. *(Up of sofa)* What's happened, Amy?

(The following is fast—but clear.)

SNAZZY. It's that Clarissa Willoughby—

AMY. She got sore—

SNAZZY. Because of what Mugsy was saying about her—

AMY. All her faults—in public—

SNAZZY. And she got into Teddy's car—

TEDDY. *(Hand to head, groaning)* I knew it! I *knew* it!

AMY. Clarissa doesn't know how to drive—

SNAZZY. She started backing up—

AMY. And I guess she couldn't stop—

SNAZZY. Anyway, she went all across your flower beds—

(MR. HUGHES *groans.*)

AMY. And across Mr. Matson's flower beds—

(MR. HUGHES *groans more loudly.*)

SNAZZY. And bang smash into a tree—

AMY. Mr. Matson's tree—

(The TELEPHONE rings.)

MR. HUGHES. Is she hurt?

TEDDY. Probably not—but think of my car!

(The TELEPHONE rings again. TEDDY, who is near it, grabs it up. The following is very fast:)

TEDDY. Hello!— *(With a growl)* Oh, it's you again, Mr. Matson. *(Listens.)*

AMY. I'm going back to see what happens next.

SNAZZY. Me, too.

AMY. *(To SNAZZY)* Are you still following me around?

(AMY *and* SNAZZY *go out up Center.*)

TEDDY. I *know* it was a good tree. It was a good car, too! *(Listens.)*

JEAN. Daddy, what are we going to do?

MR. HUGHES. *(Head in hand)* Shut up a minute. I'm thinking.

TEDDY. *(Thinking MR. HUGHES was talking to him)* What did you say, Pop?

MR. HUGHES. I said shut up!

TEDDY. Oh. *(Into telephone)* Listen, Mr. Matson, haven't we got enough trouble around here without you? My father said to shut up, he's trying to— *(Puzzled, he holds telephone away a bit)* He hung up on me.

(MRS. HUGHES and MRS. COATES appear Right. Immediately MR. HUGHES goes to MRS. HUGHES.)

MR. HUGHES. Harriet, I was never so glad to see you in my life! Listen, you've got to help me here. These kids—

MRS. HUGHES. *(With a shrug and a laugh—to MRS. COATES)* Don't mind him, Mrs. Coates. He's easily excited.

MR. HUGHES. Harriet, this place is a madhouse.

MRS. HUGHES. It seems very quiet to me.

MR. HUGHES. You just wait, Harriet.

AMY. *(Enters through French windows)* There's a man out here to see you, Dad. In his pyjamas. And his face is as red as his pyjamas.

MR. HUGHES. *(To MRS. HUGHES)* Make yourself comfortable, dear. *(Goes past AMY and out up Center.)*

TEDDY. *(To AMY)* Is Mr. Matson very big?

AMY. Who?

TEDDY. Mr. Matson—the man who wants to see Dad.

AMY. So that's who it is! Wowie! *(Disappears.)*

TEDDY. Yeah! *(He also goes out up Center.)*

MRS. HUGHES. *(Turning, somewhat embarrassed, to MRS. COATES)* Mr. Hughes always gets unduly excited over the least little thing.

MRS. COATES. Is a boy named Mike Tisdale here?

JEAN. *(Quickly)* Yes, he is. What of it?

MRS. HUGHES. *(Sharply)* Jean!

MRS. COATES. *(To MRS. HUGHES)* Then perhaps your husband is *not* unduly excited.

RUTH. *(Enters from up Center; closes door after her. To* MRS. COATES*)* Hello, Mother.

MRS. COATES. Hello, dear.

JEAN. *(Stepping up to* RUTH*)* Where's Mike?

RUTH. Mike? Oh, he went home.

JEAN. Went home!

RUTH. You didn't expect Mike to stay and face the music, did you, Jean?

MRS. COATES. *(Sitting down Right)* I'm so glad to see our daughters get along so well, Mrs. Hughes. *(*MRS. HUGHES *sits in Right Center chair)* —You know, I really don't think there'll be any difficulty at all in proposing you as a member of the Clover Club—

MRS. HUGHES. *(Excited, pleased) Really,* Mrs. Coates?

MRS. COATES. In time, my dear—of course.

JEAN. *(To* RUTH*)* I don't believe you. Mike wouldn't walk out on his own party.

(The French windows burst open and MR. HUGHES *enters—dishevelled, his hair mussed, his clothes in disarray, one hand with a handkerchief holds his mouth.* AMY *and* SNAZZY *support him, one on either side.)*

AMY. Sit down over here, Daddy.

*(*MRS. COATES *and* MRS. HUGHES *rise.* RUTH *and* JEAN *remain up of sofa.* AMY *and* SNAZZY *lead* MR. HUGHES, *who is groaning slightly, to the sofa; force him into it. During this* TEDDY *enters up Center, crosses swiftly, talking to* MR. HUGHES— *around Right end of sofa.)*

TEDDY. Why did you keep telling me to stay out? I could lick Mr. Matson myself.

MR. HUGHES. *(Taking the handkerchief away)* Then why didn't you? It's all your fault, anyway. If you'd stayed out of it, maybe I'd still have my bridge work!

(Tempo increases to Curtain.)

83

MRS. HUGHES. Jesse, what *is* the matter with you?

MRS. COATES. I never saw anything so disgusting. Never!

(MILDRED *and* CHARLES *enter from kitchen, Left.*)

MILDRED. *(At Left end of sofa—in a howl)* Daddy, what's happened?

MR. HUGHES. Mildred, don't wail like that. I can't stand that now.

CHARLES. *(Stiffly)* It appears your father has been in a fist fight.

MRS. COATES. Disgusting!

(If desired, the faces of various excited GUESTS may now appear at the French windows and remain there until end of act or the windows may open and a crowd of GUESTS gather in the background, with appropriate gestures and exclamations.)

AMY. *(To SNAZZY)* That's the kind of a friend you have! So Mike skipped out in time!

SNAZZY. *(Weakly)* Maybe he just went after some more ice cream.

TEDDY. *(To MRS. HUGHES)* He kept pushing me away, saying, "I can handle this, I can handle this." Well, he handled it— *(Pointing dramatically to MR. HUGHES)* Look at him!

MR. HUGHES. *(Mournfully)* Why doesn't everyone go away? Just go away! I've got a toothache.

(DOTTIE, SALLY *and* HOPE *appear on stairs, giggling together, unaware of the excitement.* TEDDY *turns on them and crosses to foot of stairs.)*

TEDDY. Stop that giggling! Can't you see my father's hurt!

(DOTTIE, SALLY *and* HOPE *remain on stairs.)*

CHARLES. *(To MILDRED)* Mildred, I think, under

the circumstances—I think I had better say goodnight now. *(Already he is starting across room toward hall.)*

MILDRED. Good night, Charles—

CHARLES. You know how it is—a fellow in my position—

(As he reaches hall, he is confronted by LIPSCOMB, the policeman, who grins malevolently at the room. A pause.)

LIPSCOMB. Where you think you're goin', sonny?

CHARLES. Why, I—

LIPSCOMB. Shut up and sit down some place.—That goes for all of you! *(Crosses to Center—to face MR. HUGHES)* I got a call to come out here. Disturbing the peace—breaking windows—driving a car across lawns— *(He is getting out his book)* You always looked like just the type to me—minute I laid my peepers on you. *(Bends over)* —What's the matter with your face?

MR. HUGHES. Somebody hit me.

LIPSCOMB. Serves you right. *(Looks around)* —Some party! Some crowd. Well, I got to have all your names—

JEAN. No! Don't take their names! Just mine! I'm to blame—for all of it. Because I wanted to be beautiful—because I fell in love—because I was a fool and—

AMY. *(Turning on SNAZZY again—loud)* You can just get out of here and stay out of here, Snazzy! It's not Jean's fault. It's Mike's!

TEDDY. *(Coming to Center, facing LIPSCOMB)* Listen, Mister—I'm to blame—

CHARLES. *(To MILDRED)* I never thought you came from this kind of a family.   *(WARN Curtain.)*

MILDRED. *I* don't! I mean—

MR. HUGHES. *(Standing up—unsteadily)* Come on, Officer. Let's go to jail. I need the peace.

SNAZZY. *(Who has been thinking it over)* Maybe I *am* to blame.

LIPSCOMB. Okay, okay, okay. So everybody's to blame!

JEAN. You see, at first I thought I was ugly and then I—

LIPSCOMB. *Shut up! (Slight pause)* Now let's have the names. I got a duty to do here and I don't want any more shenanigans.

CHARLES. I won't give you my name. My father—

LIPSCOMB. *(Crossing to* CHARLES*)* I'll just take your name first in that case. *(Takes him roughly by lapels)* Hurry up, pal—your name!

MILDRED. *(Wailing again)* Don't! You can't—

JEAN. *(Wildly to* LIPSCOMB*)* It's all because I wanted to be the life of the party—my own party—

CHARLES. *(A whine)* Collier—Charles Collier.

LIPSCOMB. *(Writing)* Collier— *(Seeing* MRS. COATES*)* You're next.

MRS. COATES. *(Weakly)* I think I'm going to faint—

LIPSCOMB. Well, fall the other way, Lady. Just give me your name.

JEAN. *(Loud)* Won't anyone please listen to me? Please—

(MILDRED *has rushed to* CHARLES *and is straightening his shirt;* MRS. COATES *is sinking weakly to the down Right chair;* JEAN *has leaped to stand on sofa;* MR. HUGHES *groans softly and sinks back into sofa, at Right end;* MRS. HUGHES, *torn between her husband and* MRS. COATES, *is running back and forth making ad lib exclamations;* LIPSCOMB *is writing and facing* MRS. COATES; TEDDY *is trying to administer to his father; the* GUESTS *are full of exclamations,*

AS THE CURTAIN FALLS QUICKLY

ACT THREE

SCENE: *The same.*

TIME: *The middle of the following morning.*

AT RISE: *The Hughes' household is sunk in gloom. The remains of the party are in evidence: the furniture even more disarranged than it was last evening, coke bottles everywhere, pillows in odd positions.* MRS. HUGHES, *holding an ice bag to her head and wearing a housecoat or dress, is seated in the Right Center chair. At Center* AMY *is sprawled out on the floor, the morning newspaper spread out in front of her. She wears a housecoat or robe.* MILDRED, *the picture of profound tragedy, is stretched out on the sofa, staring broodingly at the ceiling. A pause.* AMY *turns a page—with a wild rustle of paper.*

MRS. HUGHES. *(With a little groan)* Amy, do you have to turn the page so fast?

AMY. Sorry, Mother. It's continued on page five.

MILDRED. Make her stop reading about it, Mother. She's been at it for an hour.

AMY. *(Reading)* I don't want to miss any details.

MILDRED. You *know* all the details.—You were here.

AMY. *(Looking up—momentarily pleased)* This'll certainly make me popular. Just think—everybody in town is sitting around reading all about us this morning.

*(*MRS. HUGHES *groans much more audibly at this.)*

MILDRED. I think the little brat enjoys it.

AMY. You know what? We're *(She enjoys the word) notorious!*

MRS. HUGHES. Amy—you stop it. I'm going to have hysterics.

AMY. Like Mrs. Coates, you mean? Say, wasn't she a scream when she got so tough and the policeman threatened to take her down to jail overnight?

MRS. HUGHES. Amy—stop, stop it, *stop it!*

AMY. Sorry, Mother. *(A deep breath)* Well, they don't have any names in here—except ours, I mean.

MILDRED. Isn't that enough? Imagine Charles' father reading this at breakfast this morning!

AMY. Aw, don't think about Charles' father. Think about your own—standing up before a judge right this minute—trying to explain all about it—with a toothache.

MRS. HUGHES. Oh, oh, oh—!

MILDRED. Why don't you take another aspirin, Mother?

MRS. HUGHES. I've taken enough now to stop three ordinary hearts.

AMY. *(Standing up—leaving the paper on floor)* But what gripes my soul is: the first boy I ever fell in love with has to turn out to be a weak-knee. If he was a little tougher, he'd remind me of Alan Ladd.

MILDRED. *(Sneering)* Huh! If he looked a little less like a turtle, he'd remind me of Eddie Bracken.

AMY. *(Crossing to sit in Left chair)* Yeh? Well, if ever I saw a hoity-toit, it's that Charles you were with. *(Imitating)* "Mildred, I think—under the circumstances —I had better say goodnight now—"

MILDRED. Mother, listen to that! She's revolting. *(Sitting up a bit—to* AMY*)* Charles is the most popular boy in the whole Sophomore class and his father——

AMY. I know—his father's a banker. Well, Snazzy's father is a contractor. He's in an *honest* profession!

MILDRED. Mother, did you hear that?

MRS. HUGHES. Children—my head is splitting, absolutely splitting! I've never been so humiliated in my life before.

(MR. HUGHES *enters from Right. He looks as dejected as the* OTHERS, *perhaps more so. He takes off his hat as he enters.* MILDRED *sits up,* MRS. HUGHES *rises,* AMY *remains seated.)*

MR. HUGHES. *(Sardonically—as he crosses to Center)* I see my family is somewhat subdued. *(Sits on sofa next to* MILDRED*)* It's quite unusual to walk into this house and not have something flying through the air.

MRS. HUGHES. *(Rises)* Jesse—this is no time for levity. *(Steps toward* MR. HUGHES*)* What happened?

MR. HUGHES. What happened? Well, the Judge—as thin and unappetizing a character as I ever saw—read off a list of offenses as long as my arm and said, "Guilty or not guilty?"

MRS. HUGHES. What did you say?

MR. HUGHES. Well, I didn't say, *"Not* guilty."

MRS. HUGHES. You should have. Oh, Jesse, why didn't you?

MR. HUGHES. Because we *were* guilty—that's why! Then he gave me a lecture that must have lasted an hour—about how to raise a family. *(Drily)* He's a bachelor, of course.

AMY. Did you see the paper?

MR. HUGHES. I saw it.—They misspelled your mother's name. *(His hand goes to his mouth and he winces)* I've got to see a dentist—if I can afford it now.

MILDRED. Daddy, did he fine you?

MR. HUGHES. He offered to send me to jail instead. I took the fine.

MILDRED. I'll die if I have to give up my sorority!

MR. HUGHES. You might, Mildred.—Perhaps you'd rather I'd go to jail for a couple of months.

MILDRED. Of course not, Daddy—but I just *can't* give up my sorority. What about my education?

MR. HUGHES. You can get your education in the classroom. Some kids do that all the time.

MRS. HUGHES. Jesse, you're joking.

MR. HUGHES. *(Rising)* Very well—it's all a joke.

(Laughs mirthlessly) Very funny.—I may lose my job, too. Let's all have a good laugh.

MRS. HUGHES. But Jesse—you don't understand—a sorority gives a girl all the things she's supposed to get in college.

AMY. *(Cynically)* Especially a husband. *(The TELEPHONE rings. MR. HUGHES starts toward it, but pauses as AMY speaks:)* If that's the principal of the high school, we're not home.

(Again MR. HUGHES takes a step toward telephone.)

MRS. HUGHES. *(Crossing to Right)* I hope it's not Mrs. Coates—tell her I'm very ill.

(Again MR. HUGHES starts toward telephone.)

MILDRED. If it's Charles, I'll talk to him.

(By this time MR. HUGHES is almost there; he reaches for telephone.)

AMY. But if it's Snazzy, I won't!

(The TELEPHONE rings again.)

MR. HUGHES. *(Facing them a moment)* Maybe I'd better answer it anyway. *(Elaborately)* May I? *(Picks up telephone)* Hello.—Yes—speaking— Oh, yes, Mr. Nichols— Yes,.—I understand— Of course, Mr. Nichols—I can't honestly say I blame you— Goodbye.

AMY. Who's Mr. Nichols?

MR. HUGHES. *(Facing them—an expression of surrender to Fate clear on his face)* Mr. Nichols was going to rent me the building for our company. He says he can't do it now. He said he caters only to a respectable class of people.—That's not us.

MRS. HUGHES. *(Sinking to chair Right)* Jesse, what's happened to us anyway?

MR. HUGHES. *(Seriously—as he goes to Center and talks directly to MRS. HUGHES)* I'll tell you what's happened. This is the logical result of the way we've been drifting.

MRS. HUGHES. You say that as though it were my fault.

MR. HUGHES. To a certain extent, it is—and mine, too.

MRS. HUGHES. I don't know what you mean.

MR. HUGHES. Henrietta, I sincerely suggest that you start trying to figure it out.

(From upstairs there is a POUNDING on a door, very loud. ALL on stage start and look up. Then we hear SALLY's voice:)

SALLY. *(Upstairs)* Teddy Hughes, you get away from that door! I won't talk to you and I won't—

TEDDY. *(Upstairs)* Don't be so darn stubborn. If I could just kiss you once, everything'd be okay.

SALLY. *(Upstairs)* If you kiss me, I'll sue you—that's what I'll do.

MRS. HUGHES. Jesse, make them stop. Tell Sally to go back to Sheridan City— My head—

MILDRED. They've been at this all morning. Even before I was awake, Teddy was trying to slip notes under Sally's door.

(Upstairs there is the sound of a door SLAMMING. SALLY, carrying her bag, appears on the stairs and descends quickly. TEDDY, looking bedraggled and worn, wearing a robe, follows at her heels.)

TEDDY. Sally, wait a minute. We can't talk down there—

SALLY. *(To room)* Good morning.

MILDRED. Hello.

AMY. How'd you sleep?

SALLY. I slept fine. *(She is now at Center, TEDDY beside her.)*

MR. HUGHES. *(Sitting Right Center and picking up paper from floor)* That's nice, Sally.

SALLY. *(To MR. HUGHES)* How'd you sleep, Mr. Hughes?

MR. HUGHES. *(Ironically)* I had a touch of insomnia last night, Sally. I don't know why.

TEDDY. *(Reaching the breaking point)* I don't see why everybody has to be so darned polite! *(He goes up to desk and sits behind it, arms folded, morose.)*

SALLY. You know what I can't get through my head? The way this family's changed. *(To MILDRED)* You never used to be like this.

MILDRED. Why look at me?

SALLY. *(To MR. HUGHES)* Why, back in Sheridan City, you were a nice, peaceful, quiet family. What's happened to everyone?

MR. HUGHES. Don't bother your head about it, Sally. You'll soon be on your way back to Sheridan City—and you can tell all our old neighbors that as soon as we moved to Butterfield, insanity cropped up in the family.

JEAN. *(Enters at Right. She seems determined and troubled; wears a pretty, frilly dress and is without her glasses. At hall door)* Hello—

MRS. HUGHES. *(Rising)* Jean!

(SALLY *sits on Right arm of sofa.*)

AMY. Say—where the devil have you been all morning?

MR. HUGHES. Buying copies of the morning paper for your scrapbook, Jean?

JEAN. *(Advancing to near MR. HUGHES' chair)* Daddy—I was in the back of the courtroom this morning.

MR. HUGHES. You don't say? I hope you took the judge's lecture seriously.—I didn't see you.

JEAN. I slumped down so you wouldn't. I didn't want to embarrass you.

MR. HUGHES. Very thoughtful of you. I wish you'd thought of it last night.

MRS. HUGHES. Jean, we've been frantic.

JEAN. Afterward, I talked with the judge. I told him he ought to give you your money back, Daddy.

MR. HUGHES. *(With a groan)* I'll bet you made quite a hit.

JEAN. *(Sitting on arm of his chair)* No.—I just told him it was all my fault—and I told him all about the family—about Amy and Teddy and you—

TEDDY. *(Glumly)* Why didn't you leave me out of it?

JEAN. But he wouldn't give the money back.

AMY. Jean—did you know the principal telephoned this morning?

JEAN. I talked with him, too.

AMY. You talked with the principal himself?

JEAN. Sure— *(Rises)* He was very cold and gruff—you know principals—and he was trying to eat his grapefruit, but I guess I kept interrupting—

MRS. HUGHES. Jean, did you have any breakfast?

JEAN. *(Crossing to Left)* Sure. I had bacon and eggs and a lot of stuff—with the principal.

AMY. *(Loud)* You actually sat down and had breakfast with Mr. Herbert? Well, wilt my brows!

JEAN. *(Facing her parents)* Mr. Herbert said he understood perfectly—but he kept blaming you, Mother.

MRS. HUGHES. Me?

JEAN. And Daddy.

MRS. HUGHES. But I wasn't even here!

JEAN. That's why he blamed you.

TEDDY. *(Rising and coming down to Center)* I hope you left me out of that conversation. That guy doesn't like me.

JEAN. He likes you, Teddy—even if you are too typical. That's what he said you were: too typical. *(Turns to AMY)* And Mr. Herbert's especially worried about your Geometry.

AMY. *(With a shudder)* He's not the only one.

SALLY. I'm glad I'm going home today. *(Stands up)* My bus leaves in half an hour.

TEDDY. I'll take you down to the station. *(Pauses)* —I forgot—my car won't run.

SALLY. Never mind. I don't even know you, Mr. Hughes. *(Brushes by him and goes to up Center)* You may have something to talk about in here—the family, I mean. I think I'll wait in the garden. *(Directly to*

TEDDY) And I don't want anyone to follow me. *(Exits up Center.)*

TEDDY. *(Staring after her)* Holy Smoke! She walks right through me.

JEAN. Go on out, Lothario.

TEDDY. *(Puzzled)* But she said not to follow her.

JEAN. Teddy, you know less about women than I gave you credit for. If she said not to follow her, that positively means she *wants* you to follow her.

TEDDY. *(Bewildered)* Well, great jumping geraniums! How can a fellow ever know what to do?! *(He slams out up Center.)*

AMY. You know what his trouble is? He's hooked. I pity him.

JEAN. *(Quietly)* So do I.

MR. HUGHES. —By the way, Jean, where did your friend Mike disappear to last night?

JEAN. *(On guard)* He didn't disappear.

MR. HUGHES. He certainly wasn't around when it came time to take roll-call.

JEAN. *(Crossing to Center quickly to face* MR. HUGHES*)* Daddy, you're trying to fix all the blame on poor Mike, aren't you?

MR. HUGHES. Just a fair share. There's enough blame to spread it around a little.—They were Mike's friends, weren't they—not yours?

JEAN. Well, I won't stand for that! *(Angry)* You're trying to say Mike started all this. Well, it's a lot deeper than that. I talked it all over with the Judge and Mr. Herbert. Mother doesn't care what we do—she runs off to her clubs and tells us to have a good time. And you make jokes and let her get away with it. And Amy's flunking. And Teddy might be, too. And Mildred's—

MILDRED. *(Rising)* Why don't you skip me?

JEAN. *(Continuing)* Mildred's running around with a stuck-up boy that's still tied to his father's bankroll.

MILDRED. And what about Jean?

JEAN. *(Near tears now)* Me? I'm terrible! I'm the worst of the lot! I caused it all in a way. I know all about books and nothing about people and even less about myself—and—and— *(Crying)* you have to blame

Mike because that's the easy way out—when Mike's the finest, dearest boy that ever stepped into this house—I don't care what anyone says.

(Crying, she turns and stomps up the stairs, leaving them surprisedly looking after her.)

AMY. *(After a pause)* I guess we're problem children all right, aren't we? *(Rises)* I think I'll go finish dressing. *(Crossing to stairs)* Maybe I better study my Geometry, too. *(Disappears upstairs.)*

MILDRED. Everyone's been calling Charles a lot of names. *(To MR. HUGHES)* First you, then Amy, and now Jean. *(Taking a step closer)* Do you really think he *is* a snob?

MR. HUGHES. Not to mince words—yes.

MRS. HUGHES. Nonsense! He comes from one of the best families—

MR. HUGHES. Harriet— *(Rises)* that's one of the things that's the matter with you. You're becoming pretty much of a snob yourself.

MRS. HUGHES. *(Insulted and hurt)* Jesse—you've never talked to me like this before.

MR. HUGHES. I know it—and that's been one of the troubles around here.

MILDRED. *(Hesitantly)* I think I'd better—uh— *(Tiptoeing to stairs)* go—polish my nails or something. *(Goes up stairs.)*

MRS. HUGHES. *(Accusingly)* And you *know* I have a headache.

MR. HUGHES. I have a toothache, too—that makes us even. I happen to think Jean sees this thing more clearly than all of us. And now I do, too.—And that's why I'm glad all this happened.

MRS. HUGHES. Jesse, that's a horrible thing to say!

MR. HUGHES. No, sir—I mean it.—There are going to be some changes in this house. Or something drastic is going to happen.

MRS. HUGHES. *(Taken back)* Are—are you threatening to leave me?

MR. HUGHES. *(It gives him an idea)* Perhaps that *is*

what I mean. *(Walks thoughtfully to Left; turns)* Yes
—that might be exactly what I *do* mean.

MRS. HUGHES. *(Taking a few steps to Center)* You
never *did* want me in the Clover Club.

MR. HUGHES. I don't care whether you're in the
Clover Club or not. But if you'll play ball with me, I'll
get you into it—regardless of last night. Right now I'm
talking about our children. You and I are going to
start taking a greater interest in them, beinning now——

MRS. HUGHES. Do you mean you can really get me
into the Clover Club?

MR. HUGHES. *(Angry)* Harriet, have you been listening to me? Your children are more important than
any club in the world.

MRS. HUGHES. Jesse—you're still blaming me. And
I can't say I like your attitude. *(Crossing to Left, pass-
ing MR. HUGHES)* —I'm going to see about lunch.
(Exits Left.)

(MR. HUGHES *throws up his hands; shakes his head.
Then the DOORBELL rings and he crosses to
Right.)*

MR. HUGHES. Please, Heaven—— *(Eyes lifted, he disappears in hall.)*

(AMY *appears on stairs; waits a moment.* MR. HUGHES
returns with TOMMY, *who now looks rather depressed.* AMY *starts back up stairs.)*

AMY. *(Disappointed)* Oh—I was just hoping it
wouldn't be Snazzy.

MR. HUGHES. *(To* TOMMY*)* I suppose you want to
see Jean.

TOMMY. I suppose so.

MR. HUGHES. *(As he sits on Right Center chair)*
Don't you *know!*

TOMMY. Yes, I know. I'd like to see her—but I
don't think it'll do any good, do you?

MR. HUGHES. *(Kindly)* Sit down, Tommy. What's
the matter with you today? You're beginning to be as
unpredictable as everyone else.

TOMMY. *(Sitting in down Right chair)* I don't know. I guess I'm just discouraged.

MR. HUGHES. You're not alone this morning. I can tell you that.

TOMMY. Does it clear up later—when you get older, I mean? Do you get wiser—about women?

MR. HUGHES. Tommy, any man who says he's wise about women is either a darned fool or a liar.

TOMMY. Now I feel worse.

MR. HUGHES. I'm kind of baffled this morning myself—but not licked yet.—Are you?

TOMMY. Not yet—but I'm getting pretty bloody.

MR. HUGHES. I'm counting on Jean. She'll come through.

TOMMY. I'm not so sure. Maybe she really does love that swivel-tongued ape. *(Something he has been thinking)* I wish I was tougher. I've always been more interested in the laws of nature than in—oh, you know, boxing and so forth.

MR. HUGHES. Tommy, I don't think you can do it that way—by poking someone in the nose, I mean.

TOMMY. I know. I'm just thinking of the fun I could have.

MR. HUGHES. There are more subtle ways.—For instance, just now I threatened to leave Mrs. Hughes—break up the home—desert everyone.

TOMMY. *(Rising)* You *did*, Mr. Hughes?

MR. HUGHES. Sure. But do you think I mean it? It's merely strategy. Mrs. Hughes is out there now *(Points to Left)* thinking it over, wondering what I meant.—And I'm just sitting here waiting to see whether it will work.

TOMMY. *(Walking in front of* MR. HUGHES *to Left)* Well, I'll tell you: I used to have a lot of faith in that mental stuff myself. But after last night—

MR. HUGHES. Listen, Tommy—all you get out of a fist fight is a sore back or a bloody nose— *(His hand to mouth—bitterly)* or a busted bridge that cost *ninety-five dollars.*

(JEAN appears on stairs.)

97   ACT III

TOMMY. Hello, Jean.

JEAN. *(To* TOMMY*)* Oh, it's you.

MR. HUGHES. Come down, Jean. Tommy and I have been talking, and we've about decided there are some reforms needed around here.

JEAN. *(Descending)* I'll admit something's needed.

TOMMY. *(Meeting her at foot of stairs)* Who'd you think it was—Mike?

JEAN. Where'd you disappear to last night, Tommy? The policeman didn't even get your name.

TOMMY. *(Taking her wrist and swinging her around to face him)* Listen, Jean—I haven't slept all night. I think I'm in love.

JEAN. That's very interesting.—Let go my wrist.

TOMMY. I mean I'm in love with *you,* darn it!

JEAN. Oh— Don't you like it?

TOMMY. No, I hate it! I've never been so miserable!

JEAN. Where did you go last night?

TOMMY. Well, after I got sore, I climbed a tree out there to cool off. And while I was perched up there, everything happened. I had a ringside seat.

JEAN. *(Crossing to down Left)* I hope you were amused.

TOMMY. *(Following her)* What I liked the most was the way Mike skipped through the hedge and down the alley when the trouble started.

JEAN. I'll wait until I hear Mike's version. *(Sits on Left end of sofa.)*

(MRS. HUGHES *enters from Left; crosses to sit at desk during following.)*

TOMMY. All right, wait! I used to think you were a smart girl. Now you're acting just like all the others. *(Tragically)* The only trouble is: I fell for you in the meantime. Darn, darn, *darn!*

JEAN. *(With irony)* That's the most romantic speech I've ever heard.

TOMMY. *(At Center)* I don't care what it sounds like. You don't know what happens to me when I get mad.

JEAN. I saw you last night. You said: "Wise men win because they use mental means and they keep their heads." Then you chewed up a table leg and went off to pout.

MR. HUGHES. *(Crossing to* MRS. HUGHES, *who is going through papers on desk)* Well, Harriet—have you thought over what I said?

MRS. HOLMES. *(Betraying nothing)* I'm looking for a recipe.

JEAN. Everyone seems to be picking on Mike this morning. But it doesn't matter to me. I'll stick by him, I don't care what anyone says.

(The DOORBELL rings. JEAN *crosses toward Right, but as she reaches hall* MIKE *appears, not having waited for anyone to open the door for him.)*

MIKE. *(All smiles) Good* morning! How's everyone this swell morning?

JEAN. *(Hands on hips)* You've certainly got a nerve coming here this morning, Mr. Michael Tisdale!

TOMMY. *(Puzzled)* But Jean, you just said—

JEAN. *(Snappily to* TOMMY, *over her shoulder)* Never mind what I just said. *(To* MIKE*)* You've got the quaintest kind of nerve to show up here this morning after what you did last night!

MR. HUGHES. *(Crossing to behind* TOMMY *and placing a hand on his shoulder)* Don't try to figure it out, Tommy. It's too deep for the mind of man. *(Goes to French windows)* I'm going next door to apologize to Mr. Matson. I've decided he was perfectly justified— even if I do have to eat nothing but soup for a couple of weeks. *(Hand to jaw, turns at French windows)* —Remember, Tommy—the mind is stronger than the stiffest right hook in existence. *(Goes out.)*

TOMMY. He's a brave man. *(Stepping up to* JEAN*)* —Well, maybe you have gotten some sense after all. *(To* MIKE*)* Jean's perfectly right, Tisdale.

MIKE. *(Disgruntled)* What do you know about it, Steinie?

JEAN. *(Another complete change—to* TOMMY'S *utter*

99   ACT III

bewilderment) Mike— *(Her voice dripping honey, she takes* MIKE's *arm)* come over here and sit down and tell me what happened. *(Leading him to sofa—past an amazed and lost* TOMMY*)* Everyone keeps asking. Did you go after some more refreshments?

(JEAN *and* MIKE *sit on sofa.)*

TOMMY. *(Stuttering)* But Jean—you just said—I thought you meant—don't you really think— *(Giving it up with something approaching a yelp)* —What am I doing here anyway? What does it all mean? Jean, you just said—

MIKE. *(To* JEAN*)* What's come over Steinie now?

TOMMY. *(Trembling with rage, goes down to face* MIKE*) You better stop calling me Steinie!* Do you hear that, Tisdale? *Never—call—me—Steinie—again!*

MIKE. Okay, Steinie, I promise.

TOMMY. *(Throwing himself helplessly into the Right Center chair)* You wait. You just wait! Your time's coming! *(Half to himself)* I've got to keep my head— mental means—keep my head and use mental means— mind stronger than the stiffest right hook in existence—

AMY. *(Comes tearing down the stairs again, pausing at bottom and talking as she comes)* I saw Mike's car out front. Is Snazzy with you, Mike? *(Crosses to Center)* I hope not!

MIKE. Why not?

AMY. Because if he isn't, it might prove he's wising up!

SNAZZY. (SNAZZY's *head appears, peering around door from hall. In a little voice—tentatively)* Hi-ya, Amy—

AMY *(Turning on him with a moan)* Oh! I might have known!

SNAZZY. You feel any better this morning, Amy?

AMY. *(A few steps toward him)* Snazzy, you disgust me!

(The DOORBELL rings.)

JEAN. Get it, Amy.

AMY. *(Crossing to hall)* Everybody in town meets at the Hughes'. *(Exits into hall.)*

SNAZZY. *(Wandering up to desk)* Good morning, Mrs. Hughes.

MRS. HUGHES. How do you do? Aren't you the boy that fainted the other evening? How do you feel now?

(SNAZZY goes to sit on hassock. AMY returns, followed by CHARLES COLLIER. CHARLES wears an expression of thin-lipped determination, not very pleasant.)

AMY. *(As they come in—not too pleasantly)* I'll call her. *(Crosses to stairs; calls up)* Mildred! *Mildred!* Mr. Collier calling.

CHARLES. Thank you. *(To MRS. HUGHES)* How do you do, Mrs. Hughes?

(MRS. HUGHES nods and CHARLES crosses down Right.)

MIKE. *(To JEAN)* Can't we have any privacy, Jean?

TOMMY. *(Quickly)* What do you want privacy for?

JEAN. *(To MIKE)* Wait a minute. I want to see this.

(MILDRED descends the stairs, a bit too quickly. AMY remains at foot of stairs and MILDRED crosses to CHARLES.)

MILDRED. *(Coolly—as though waiting for something)* Good morning, Charles.

CHARLES. Good morning, Mildred. May I—uh—that is, do you suppose we could go out into the garden?

MILDRED. I'm afraid my brother is using the garden at the moment. Is it something you can't say here?

CHARLES. Well—

TOMMY. *(Recklessly—with a wave of the hand)* Go ahead, Charlie. Go right ahead. All the rest of us do. *(Rises and crosses to sit on stairs.)*

CHARLES. Well—it *is* rather private. I mean to say, of course—

MILDRED. Yes, Charles?

(MR. HUGHES returns, standing just inside French windows, listening.)

CHARLES. It's only that I—and my father, of course —have been reading the morning paper. And—well, we were pleased to see that the names of the—er—guests did not appear. My father wants to know—and I want to know: are they likely to appear in the afternoon papers? You know, in my position—

MILDRED. *(Very cold)* I assure you, Mr. Collier, you have nothing to worry about. We have done all in our power to keep the papers from getting the names.—But I had hoped that you had a less selfish reason for coming to see me. *(Slight pause)* Goodbye.

CHARLES. "Goodbye?"

MILDRED. *(More and more angry—controlling herself)* You'd better get out of here, Charles Collier.

CHARLES. Say—you can't throw me out of here like that. What do you think this place is? After what I saw here last night—

MILDRED. *(Reaching for a vase sitting on the desk)* You better get out of here fast, you snob, you— *(She raises the vase as though to hurl it.)*

(CHARLES cringes. MRS. HUGHES half rises and screams.)

AMY. Let him have it, Mildred!

CHARLES. *(Cringing, frightened, confused)* What's the matter with you anyway?

(MILDRED makes a still more threatening gesture and CHARLES disappears in hall. MILDRED lowers the vase.)

MRS. HUGHES. Mildred, that's my best vase.

CHARLES. *(CHARLES' head appears around door)* I just want to say I think the whole family's crazy!

(CHARLES disappears and MILDRED hurls the vase; it goes through door and crashes offstage; the outside DOOR slams off Right.)

MR. HUGHES. *(Crossing to* JEAN*)* Congratulations, daughter. There are more subtle ways, but I agree with the essence of what you—

MILDRED. *(Turning on him)* Oh, leave me alone! Leave me alone! *(In tears)* I hate him, the simpering little snob—but I love him, too. What do you think of that?! *(Crossing swiftly to stairs.* TOMMY *gets out of her way)* And now it'll be all over college! Sometimes I wish I was dead! *(Disappears upstairs with a wail.)*

(They ALL *look after her.)*

TOMMY. *(The first to speak)* Maybe all women are alike.—I'm going to get trampled on these stairs. *(Sits again.)*

AMY. Imagine! All he cared about was whether his name would get into the paper. He didn't care at all about poor Mildred.

MR. HUGHES. —Well, I had a talk with Mr. Matson. He's really a very reasonable man. And he even has a building he'll rent me— *(With a significant look toward* MRS. HUGHES*)* if I decide to stay here at all.

JEAN. *(Alarmed—rising)* Daddy, what do you mean?

(The DOORBELL rings again.)

AMY. *(As she goes)* I hope it's just a peddler. *(Exits in hall.)*

MIKE. You know, a house like this would make me nervous. All these people all the time.

JEAN. *(Crossing to* MR. HUGHES *at Center)* Daddy— what did you mean: "If I decide to stay here at all"?

(Before MR. HUGHES *can answer,* AMY *returns with* MRS. COATES. MRS. COATES *is in one of her less pleasant moods this morning: her chin set, her eyes narrow, her voice cold.* JEAN *goes to upstage of sofa.)*

AMY. Mother—Mrs. Coates to see you. *(Remains just inside Right door.)*

MRS. HUGHES. Good morning, Mrs. Coates. *(Rises and comes around desk to meet* MRS. COATES *between Right and Right Center chairs.)*

MRS. COATES. I didn't come to see you, Mrs. Hughes. I came to see whether my daughter Ruth was here.

MRS. HUGHES. No, she isn't, Mrs. Coates. I haven't seen her this morning.

MR. HUGHES. But everyone else is here. Take your pick.

MRS. COATES. Because if she were, I wanted to take her home. I've forbidden her to enter this house. *(Sees* MIKE*)* —I'm pleased to see you here, Mike. Maybe you'll stay away from my daughter now.

MRS. HUGHES. *(Defensively)* What's the matter with this house, Mrs. Coates?

MRS. COATES. We won't go into that.

MR. HUGHES. *(Stepping between them)* Mrs. Coates —have you seen the paper this morning?

MRS. COATES. Disgraceful!

MR. HUGHES. Indeed it is. And we're awfully sorry it happened. But all day the newspapers have been after me to give them the names of the people at the party.

MRS. COATES. Oh, Mr. Hughes—you wouldn't do that!

MR. HUGHES. *(Significantly)* I haven't—yet.

MRS. COATES. What do you mean?

MR. HUGHES. Well, Mrs. Coates, I can't punch you in the eye—even if it would make me feel good—so I've resorted to other means.

MRS. COATES. I think I see. You sound like a black-mailer to me. And furthermore, I don't believe you.

(The TELEPHONE rings.)

MR. HUGHES. Pardon me. *(Goes to answer telephone)* Hello.—Yes— No— No— No! *(Hangs up)* *The Evening World.* Wanted a story. *(Returns to* MRS. COATES*)* Do you believe me now?

MRS. COATES. *(Turning to* MRS. HUGHES, *sweetly)* Mrs. Hughes, you'll believe me when I say I had absolutely no intention of changing my plans. At the very next meeting of the Clover Club—

MRS. HUGHES. I think I'll wait a while, Mrs. Coates —thank you. I've decided to wait until my children are a little older.

MRS. COATES. You mean—?

MRS. HUGHES. *(Taking* MR. HUGHES' *hand)* I belong to too many clubs already. Perhaps some other time.

MRS. COATES. Well— *(Uncertainly)* then—I suppose all is forgiven and forgotten. *(With an insincere little chuckle)* All little mistakes, you know—we all make them. *(Moves to hall Right)* Goodbye now. *(Very sweet indeed—with a little wave of her hand)* Goodbye, everyone. *(Disappears in hall.)*

TOMMY. Mr. Hughes—that's using the head.

JEAN. Daddy—who called?

MR. HUGHES. *(Surprised)* By Jove, it worked.

JEAN. Did *The Evening World* really call?

MR. HUGHES. *(Chuckling)* It was someone for Mildred. I had to take a chance.

MRS. HUGHES. *(Smiling)* Jesse, you're an old fraud!

MR. HUGHES. I'm not so old.

(RUTH COATES *enters from up Center.)*

RUTH. May I come in?

JEAN. *(Goes up Center)* By all means. I've been waiting to see you.

MR. HUGHES. All things come to him who waits—in this house. *(To* MRS. HUGHES) —What about that lunch, Harriet? Need any help?

MRS. HUGHES. Come along, Jesse. *(Holding hands, they exit Left.)*

AMY. They were holding hands! I never saw them holding hands before in my life!

RUTH. I've been waiting for Mother to leave.

SNAZZY. Amy—I've been thinking—

AMY. Are you still here?

SNAZZY. *(Crossing to* AMY) What do you want me to do, anyway? I'll do anything. I'm desperate! Love makes you desperate.

RUTH. *(As she comes around Right end of sofa and faces MIKE)* I might have known I'd find you *here.*

AMY. *(To SNAZZY)* How desperate? I think Mike owes us all an apology.

MIKE. *(To RUTH, rising)* I just dropped by to see how everything was, that's all, Ruth.

SNAZZY. All right! *(Making a decision and drawing himself up as he turns to the room)* If that's what you want—that's what you get!

RUTH. *(To MIKE)* And how did you find everything?

JEAN. *(Coming around Left end of sofa and facing RUTH across MIKE)* Ruth—do you always follow Mike —wherever he goes?

SNAZZY. *(Stepping down to face MIKE across RUTH)* Mike, did you hear what Amy said?

MIKE. Now, Ruth—I wish you'd—

SNAZZY. *(Raising his voice)* Mike! *Did you hear what Amy said?*

MIKE. *(To SNAZZY)* No—and what's more, I don't care a darn what Amy said! *(To RUTH)* Ruth, I only want to say—

SNAZZY. *(Even louder)* You'd better listen better when Amy talks, Mike! Amy said she thinks everyone here deserves an apology—and so do I.

MIKE. Oh, you do? Well, you just shut up and let me talk to Ruth—

SNAZZY. You can talk to Ruth as soon as you apologize.

MIKE. *(To RUTH)* Pardon me. *(To JEAN)* Pardon me. *(Crosses in front of RUTH to face SNAZZY)* This won't take a minute. *(Grabs SNAZZY's tie and twists it hard. In a low, threatening voice)* —Can't you hear me talking to these girls? What's the idea of interrupting me when I'm holding a conversation? Now go outside for a while.

AMY. *(To MIKE—angrily)* Who do you think you are—Humphrey Bogart?

SNAZZY. Let go of my tie, Mike.

MIKE. Will you go outside like I asked you to? Like a good little boy.

SNAZZY. Sure I'll go outside. Come on out in the garden. *(Puts up his fists.)*

MIKE. Snazzy, I could break you in two.

AMY. Sock him, Snazzy!

SNAZZY. You better let go my necktie, Mike—I'm warning you!

(TOMMY comes to Left end of sofa and watches.)

MIKE. I'll let go as soon as you get outside and stay outside.

AMY. *(Her cheer)* "Eat 'em up, chew 'em up, spit 'em out—Bulldogs!"

SNAZZY. All right, Mike—you asked for it.

(He throws back an arm and hits MIKE on the nose with his fist. MIKE howls once and releases SNAZ-ZY's necktie.)

MIKE. Why, you hit me! *(Starts after SNAZZY threateningly.)*

AMY. Hit him again, Snazzy! I love you, boy! Hit him again!

MIKE. You're looking for a fight—you're going to get a fight!

(He begins to back SNAZZY around the sofa. By this time SNAZZY is pretty frightened; he backs up slowly, MIKE right after him.)

MIKE. I ought to lay you out cold—

(Above the sofa, SNAZZY picks up the hassock, holds it in front of him like a bullfighter with his cape— and SNAZZY begins to talk as MIKE presses him around Left arm of sofa to a position near down Left chair.)

SNAZZY. You can lick me, Mike. But you can't keep me from *talking!* *(In a hurry, as MIKE makes a grab for him)* I remember a lot of things, too. I remember who put the dead cat in the ventilating system at school—

MIKE. *(Knowing he is caught)* Snazzy! *(His arms, formerly in a fighting position, drop to his side)* Snazzy, you wouldn't do that!

SNAZZY. You've deserved that punch in the nose for a long time.

MIKE. If you ever told all that—

SNAZZY. *(Victorious)* I wouldn't hesitate a minute.

MIKE. *(Defeated)* Okay— *(Baffled)* Okay. You win.

RUTH. Serves you right. You've always pushed everyone around, Mike.

JEAN. Well, he didn't push *me* around! *(Takes MIKE's arm)* I did exactly what I wanted to do all the time.

TOMMY. *(Coming down to between MIKE and SNAZZY—to SNAZZY)* That's using the head, Snazz.

SNAZZY. *(Setting hassock on floor and dusting off his hands)* Thanks, Tommy. *(Crosses to AMY at Right)* —Is that what you wanted, Amy?

AMY. I didn't hear him apologize.

JEAN. Oh, Amy, let's drop this foolishness.

SNAZZY. *(To MIKE)* Yeah—we haven't heard you apologize yet.

MIKE. Well, wait a minute, can't you? Things are happening too fast around here—and my sinus trouble's starting. *(Hand to nose.)*

SNAZZY. We're still waiting.

MIKE. All right, all right. I'm sorry. You want me to get on my knees?

AMY. *(To SNAZZY, throwing her arms around him)* Snazzy—you're wonderful!

SNAZZY. *(Riding the crest)* Then kiss me.

AMY. I will not! It's against our rules.

SNAZZY. *(Tough now, and sure of himself)* Kiss me, I said!

AMY. But I'm a *Slick*. I can't kiss.

SNAZZY. When I say kiss me, I mean kiss me.

(He takes AMY into his arms and kisses her before she can protest further. When he releases her, she smiles at him.)

AMY. *(In a breath)* Alan Ladd!

TOMMY. *(To RUTH)* —Ruth, you know what I think? Why don't we get out of here? *(Crosses to her)* If you don't have any other plans, why don't we go for a picnic this afternoon and then a movie tonight?

RUTH. Well, Tommy—that sounds like a grand idea!

MIKE. Hey, wait a minute.

TOMMY. *(To RUTH)* What's the matter with him?

MIKE. *(To TOMMY)* Now get this straight, Steinie— I've had about enough—about all I'm going to take around here. Last night was very hard on me and today hasn't been any better. So you just start being careful—

TOMMY. *(To RUTH)* What's he talking about? Do you have any idea?

RUTH. None. *(Slipping an arm through TOMMY's)* —I'll borrow my brother's convertible and we'll drive out to Pleasantview Park—

MIKE. Ruth, you're not going with this guy?

RUTH. And why not?

MIKE. Because I say not! You can't start pulling that stuff on me. I don't like it.

JEAN. Never mind, Mike—we'll have a picnic ourselves.

MIKE. *(To JEAN)* Now, Jean, you stay out of this.

RUTH. What stuff? I don't know what you're talking about.

MIKE. You certainly do—

JEAN. I will not stay out of it. You've brought me into it and I intend to stay.

MIKE. *(To RUTH)* If you go with this grease-ball, it's the end. Get that—the end!

RUTH. *(Cheerfully)* Very well. It's the end. Coming, Tommy?

MIKE. *(Changing his tune)* Aw now, Ruth—*please!*

TOMMY. *(To JEAN)* You and Mike have a good time. You can help him with his Latin.

MIKE. Ruth, you know there's no one in the world but you. You know—

JEAN. That's not what you told me last night.

RUTH. What *did* he tell you last night?

JEAN. He said——

MIKE. Jean,—Holy Mackeral!—will you keep out of this? *(To* RUTH*)* You know why I played my cards the way I did. You wanted to have the party as much as I did, didn't you?

TOMMY. And this was the only place in town where you could have your party. Well, you had it. I had a good time myself. But now it's over. *(To* RUTH*)* —I've never driven a convertible before.

MIKE. *(Desperate)* Holy Mackeral, you get me mixed up!

JEAN. *(To* TOMMY—*as she crosses to him)* Tommy, what did you mean—"This was the only place in town Mike could have his party"?

TOMMY. Did I say that?

JEAN. You mean everyone else was too smart for him—

MIKE. *(To* JEAN*)* Now, Jean, be reasonable. You know you're the brightest girl in school.

TOMMY. That's right, Jean—bright but not beautiful. Quite a set-up for Mike. Glasses, sloppy clothes, unpopular—a perfect set-up.

MIKE. Steinie, I've taken about all I'm going to take —I warn you!

JEAN. A perfect set-up—me? *(She has begun to get it: her face has a stricken look.)*

MIKE. But that's not true! I think you *are* beautiful, Jean. The way you blossomed out—

RUTH. That's all I wanted to know. *(Takes a step toward Right door.)*

MIKE. *(To* RUTH—*quickly)* But for Pete's sake, Ruth—you know I don't care about anyone but you. —And if you let Steinie drive that car—

JEAN. I see now. *(Very quietly)* I see. So Mike turned on the charm—and simple little Cinderella fell— Isn't that true, Mike?

MIKE. No, it's not. I like you, Jean, only—

JEAN. *(Softly)* Sure, I get it. What a little idiot! *(To* RUTH*)* —Take him away, Ruth. *(She is holding back real tears)* Go on, both of you—please.

RUTH. *(Going to* JEAN*)* I'm sorry, Jean.

JEAN. Never mind. *(To* MIKE*)* —Was I very funny,

Mike? Did I make you laugh? I hope you enjoyed yourself. *(To* RUTH *again)* —Take him away, Ruth, will you? *(Desperate to conceal her feelings)* Right away.

MIKE. Jean, honest—I didn't mean to hurt you. You just took it all so seriously and——

JEAN. If you don't get out of here this minute, I'm going to cry. And I don't—want you to—see me crying.

RUTH. *(To* MIKE*)* Come on, Drip. I don't know why I put up with you. *(Leading him toward Right door)* Maybe some day you'll develop a brain to go with that charm—but I doubt it.

*(*MIKE *and* RUTH *disappear in hall. A moment.* ALL *are watching* JEAN, *sympathizing.)*

TOMMY. I'm sorry, Jean. *(Crossing to her)* It was just something that had to be done. They call it being cruel in order to be kind.

JEAN. *(To* TOMMY*)* You planned it this way! Tommy, you planned to make Mike admit that! That's why you started asking Ruth for a date.

TOMMY. Maybe I shouldn't've done it.

JEAN. *(Quietly)* I hate you, Tommy. I hate you. I was so happy before.

*(*MR. *and* MRS. HUGHES *enter from Left. They also are sober.* MR. HUGHES *goes to* JEAN.*)*

MR. HUGHES. We heard it in the kitchen, Jean. *(Hand on her shoulder)* We're sorry—

TOMMY. *(To* MR. HUGHES*)* Well, I used my head—or did I? *(*JEAN *moves slowly, like a blind person, to the desk)* —Jean, you might like to know my reason. It was because I do care for you—really care. And I knew all along—

JEAN. *(Picks up her glasses and slowly puts them on again)* You've been very considerate—all of you. Knowing what a fool I was—I mean *am*—and being so kind—while I kicked up my heels—while I played belle of the ball—life of the party— *(Bitterly as she goes to stairs)* Some party! *(Without breaking down, but with a definite suggestion of tears, she exits upstairs.)*

TOMMY. *(Bitterly as he crosses and drops into Right chair)* Yeh—I used my head.

(The TELEPHONE rings. AMY crosses and answers it.)

AMY. Hello— Just a moment, please. *(Crosses to stairs and calls up)* —Mildred! Telephone!

MRS. HUGHES. I don't think Mildred will be able to talk. She was feeling pretty bad when she went upstairs.

MILDRED. *(Upstairs)* Is it Charles?

AMY. He says his name's MacKenzie.

MILDRED. *(Appearing on stairs, excited and radiant —without a trace of a tear)* MacKenzie! *(Very excited, as she tromps down)* Mac! The captain of the football team himself! The most popular boy in the whole Senior class! *(Reaches telephone and answers— her voice dripping syrup)* Hel-lo, Mac— *(She sinks to the chair behind desk and continues a low conversation under following.)*

SNAZZY. *(To AMY, crossing to her at foot of stairs)* Amy—you know, there's just one thing that bothers me.

AMY. What's that, Snazz?

SNAZZY. Well, I don't like to say it, but I'm not the type of a fellow that likes to go around with a girl who's flunking her Geometry.

AMY. I won't flunk now, Snazzy—with you to help me.

SNAZZY. *(Beaming)* Well, I guess everything's okay, then.

(TEDDY and SALLY enter up Center, hand in hand, eyes full of lovelight.)

TEDDY. *(Going Right Center with SALLY)* Sally and I have reached an agreement.

SALLY. *(All sweetness)* Yes, we have.

MR. HUGHES. Get it in black and white, Sally.

TEDDY. Sally convinced me I was wrong.

SALLY. I had to slap his face twice, though.

TEDDY. *(For the sake of the record)* Once. I caught your wrist the second time.

SALLY. *(Fondly)* He's very persuasive.

TEDDY. *(To* MR. HUGHES) Pop, you can stop worrying about little Teddy right now. From now on I'm putting all my eggs in one basket.

MILDRED. *(Her voice rising)* But of course I would, Mac. I'd *love* to!

MR. HUGHES. *(Going Left to* MRS. HUGHES)) I'm more worried about Jean than anything. I think she's been more badly scorched than anyone in this whole affair.

TOMMY. *(Rising)* Mr. Hughes—

MR. HUGHES. Yes, Tommy?

TOMMY. Maybe I shouldn't've told her. Maybe people are always happier if they're kidding themselves.

MR. HUGHES. I'm hoping it's her pride that's hurt most. I'm hoping she—

(He breaks off as JEAN *appears on stairs. She wears slacks and a shirt—but now the shirt fits and the slacks are more attractive. Her hair is still loose and pretty, but she wears her glasses—but now the rims, instead of being dark, are pink, the same color as her fingernail polish. She has in her arms a stack of library books.)*

AMY. Jean, you colored your glasses!

JEAN. I feel better with them on. I can see better.

AMY. They match your fingernails!

MR. HUGHES. You look very nice, Daughter.

MRS. HUGHES. Very nice, Jean.

TOMMY. Swell—not too much, not too little. Just yourself!

JEAN. *(On stairs)* Tommy—

TOMMY. *(Taking a step—excited)* Yes, Jean—?

JEAN. Do you want to go to the library with me?

TOMMY. *(Getting flustered—in all directions)* Go to the lib—go to the library with you? Sure! Let's go! *(Crosses excitedly to* MR. HUGHES) —She wants me

to go with her—Jean wants me to go with her—!!
(Crossing to SNAZZY) —Hear that? *(Crossing to
stairs)* —Sure I want to go. Let's get going. I mean—
you forgive me, Jean?

JEAN. I'm grateful to you, Tommy.

TOMMY. *(Almost too much joy to bear)* Grateful to
me?!! Hear that—she's grateful to me! Oh, man! Oh,
golly—!

MR. HUGHES. Remember, Tommy: wise men keep
their heads.

TOMMY. Keep my head—that's right. Gotta keep my
head. *(To* JEAN) Give me the books— (JEAN *hands
books to* TOMMY, *who starts having difficulty with them
because he is so nervous)* Have to keep my—oh, boy,
are you beautiful, Jean?! Oh, boy, are you— *(Drops a
book in his excitement)* Dropped it. *(Stoops)* I'll get it.
Hold everything now—I'll— *(Stands up)* Got it. All
ready? *(Having great difficulty with books)* Kind of
nervous, I guess. *(Drops another book as he and* JEAN
start to Right) Dropped another one. *(Sheepishly)* I'll
get it. *(Stoops.)*

*(From off Right there comes a tremendous CRASH—
as of two cars smashing up—same effect as in Act
Two.* ALL *start.)*

AMY. What was that?   *(WARN Curtain.)*

TOMMY. *(Standing up again)* Did you hear that?

MR. HUGHES. What the—?

TEDDY. *(Loud)* My car! That sounded just like my
car.

(From Right LIPSCOMB *enters. Instead of his usual
gruff and self-important self, he is considerably
abashed, nervous, ashamed. As* TEDDY *dashes to
Right,* LIPSCOMB *meets him at hall entrance. At
sight of* LIPSCOMB, *there is a general reaction:* MR.
HUGHES *groans,* AMY *mumbles "Here we go
again," etc.)*

LIPSCOMB. Now take it easy, Son. I'll take care of
all of it. Just a little mistake.

MR. HUGHES. What happened?

LIPSCOMB. Well, it was this way—I was driving by —and I got to looking into the house to see what was happening this morning and I guess I wasn't looking where I was going—

TEDDY. My car!

MR. HUGHES. *(Loud) No! (Sinks to sofa.)*

MRS. HUGHES. *(In a screech)* Don't tell me—!!

LIPSCOMB. I smashed right into it out there at the curb. *(The Curtain has begun to fall)* But don't you worry. I'll pay for everything. I don't want you to report me, that's all. It could happen to anyone—

(TEDDY *is repeating:* "My car, my car!" JEAN *has taken* TOMMY'S *arm.* MRS. HUGHES *sits slowly in Left chair. The* OTHERS *crowd around* LIPSCOMB, *who continues to apologize profusely as*

THE CURTAIN FALLS

LIFE OF THE PARTY

NOTE

Most amateur productions are marred to a greater or less degree by the fact that the actors do not wait for laughs. The trick is to wait for the laugh to reach a peak, then begin to subside, before the next line is spoken. The trick is complicated because the actor must also be careful not to let this slow the tempo; that is, he must not wait *too long*. The success or failure in this one detail is sometimes the key to the success or failure of the production.

LIFE OF THE PARTY

PROPERTY PLOT

Decorative Properties:
  Trellis
  Books in case
  Books, magazines, vase with flowers—on library
    table
  Bowls of fruit, candy dish
  Pillows
  Pictures on wall
  Photographs on radio
  Drapes on French windows
 Add at beginning of Act II:
  Chinese lanterns strung on trellis
 Add at beginning of Act III:
  Coke bottles
Set Properties:
  Straight chair
  Bookcase
  Radio
  Hassock
  Desk
  Straight chair
  Telephone
  Lounge chair
  Lounge chair and ottoman
  Sofa
  Library table

HAND PROPERTIES

Act One:
  Pipe, Mr. Hughes
  Newspaper, Mr. Hughes

Book in bright dust jacket, MRS. HUGHES
Horn-rimmed glasses, JEAN
Book, JEAN
Apple, JEAN
Billfold, MR. HUGHES
Books, MILDRED
Watch, MR. HUGHES
Hair curlers, MRS. HUGHES

Act Two:
Hair curlers, AMY
Evening gown, AMY
Corsage—box and flowers, MR. HUGHES
Evening gown, JEAN
Towel, JEAN
Three or four bills, MR. HUGHES
Matches, MR. HUGHES
Corsage in box, CHARLES COLLIER
Large bowl of potato chips, JEAN
Golf bag and clubs, SNAZZY
Overnight case, SALLY
Golf bag and clubs, MR. HUGHES
Handkerchief, MR. HUGHES
Notebook and pencil, LIPSCOMB

Act Three:
Ice bag, MRS. HUGHES
Newspaper, AMY
Hat, MR. HUGHES
Overnight case, SALLY
Robe, TEDDY
Papers and letters (on desk), MRS. HUGHES
Vase on desk, MILDRED
Hassock, SNAZZY
Glasses, JEAN
Glasses (rims tinted same as fingernails), JEAN
Five or six library books, JEAN

LIFE OF THE PARTY

SOUND EFFECT CUES

Act One:

Cue: MRS. HUGHES—"If I do say so myself."
From upstairs comes a loud banging of fists on
a door.

CUE: TEDDY—"Oh, all right."
A door bangs upstairs.

Cue: AMY—"And do you smell sweet! Wow!"
The door bangs again.

Cue: TEDDY—"I'm gonna write her a letter."
The doorbell rings.

Cue: MILDRED—"Everyone's always picking on
me!"
The door slams upstairs.

Cue: JEAN—"Just a—a—a dull tone!"
The door slams.

Cue: MR. HUGHES—"A psychological study of the
modern parent."
The doorbell rings.

Cue: TEDDY—"Terrible ordeal. Terrible."
The front door slams.

Cue: MIKE—"That's a sweetheart!"
The front door slams.

Cue: SNAZZY—"Whee!"
Front door slams.

Cue: MRS. HUGHES—"Be sure to invite—"
The front door slams.

Cue: JEAN—"Don't call me a liar!"
The telephone rings.

Act Two:

Cue: MRS. HUGHES—"Jesse! Don't you dare."
The doorbell rings.

Cue: AMY—"He's combed his hair seven times!"
The door slams upstairs.
Cue: MR. HUGHES—"Have you ever seen me eat
peas with a knife?"
The door slams upstairs.
Cue: MR. HUGHES—". . . caught right smack in
the middle of this whole crazy business."
The front door bell rings.
Cue: TEDDY—" 'Bye."
The front door slams.
Cue: MILDRED—"You'll love him."
The doorbell rings.
Cue: TOMMY—". . . and one of these days—"
The doorbell rings.
Cue: MR. HUGHES—"I'm head doorman here to-
night."
The outside door is heard to open.
Cue: TOMMY—"*Your* party?"
The doorbell rings.
Cue: MIKE—"Sorry—I gotta go, sorry."
Door slams.
Cue: MR. HUGHES—"Lordy, I'm glad I'm an old
man."
Radio music is heard from the garden.
Cue: DOTTIE—"Where do you get that 'dear'
stuff anyway, Shuttleworth?"
Telephone rings.
Cue: TEDDY—"Shhh—!"
Telephone rings again.
Cue: RUTH—"That's the scientific mind at work."
There is a crash outside—glass smashing.
Cue: JEAN—"Maybe Tommy tried to cool himself
off in the punchbowl."
Doorbell rings.
Cue: SNAZZY—"Tell everyone to go home."
Telephone rings.
Cue: MARYROSALIE—"And my brother's a Golden
Gloves champion!"
The outside door slams.
Cue: MR. HUGHES—"Let me have some of it."

Crash from garden—breaking glass, smashing fender, etc.

Cue: AMY—"Mr. Matson's tree."

The telephone rings.

Cue: TEDDY—"Probably not, but think of my car!"

The telephone rings again.

Act Three:

Cue: AMY—"Especially a husband."

The telephone rings.

Cue: AMY—"But if it's Snazzy, I won't!"

The telephone rings again.

Cue: MR. HUGHES—"Henrietta, I sincerely suggest that you start trying to figure it out."

From upstairs there is a loud pounding on a door.

Cue: MILDRED—". . . to sleep notice Sally's door."

Upstairs the door slams.

Cue: MRS. HUGHES—"—I'm going to see about lunch."

The doorbell rings.

Cue: JEAN—". . . I don't care what anyone says!"

The doorbell rings.

Cue: AMY—"Snazzy, you disgust me!"

The doorbell rings.

Cue: CHARLES—"I think the whole family's crazy!"

Door slams off Right.

Cue: JEAN—"Daddy, what do you mean?"

The doorbell rings again.

Cue: MRS. COATES—"I don't believe you."

The telephone rings.

Cue: TOMMY—"Yeah—I used my head."

The telephone rings.

Cue: TOMMY—"I'll find it."

From off Right there comes a tremendous crash, as of two cars smashing up.

SOUND EFFECT EQUIPMENT

Doorbell.
Telephone bell.

Slam door.
Glass to smash.
Record of dance music to play offstage.
Tin to crush, as of fenders smashing.

NOTES ON LIGHTS

Acts One and Two use general lighting for evening inside. In Act Two after the curtain has been lowered and raised to denote passing of a few hours, lighted Chinese lanterns are hung from the trellis. In all the night scenes, a moonlight (blue flood or spot) may be used effectively in the garden, flowing across the French windows and spilling onto stage when windows are open. General daylight effects with sun coming in from the French windows are used in Act Three. There are no light problems involved and no light cues within the scenes.

NOTES ON COSTUMES

Attractive spring clothes may be worn in Act One and in Act Three. Evening gowns of various colors will add to the charm of Act Two. Tuxedoes may or may not be worn by the boys in Act Two.

LIFE OF THE PARTY

PUBLICITY

The ——————— Players of ——————— will present
Life of the Party, a new comebdy by Marrijane and
Joseph Hayes, on ——————— evening, at ———————
o'clock.

If you enjoy watching gay, charming people enacting
a lively story of modern youth and family life, come
and meet the Hughes family. They have just moved to
Butterfield where they make new friends and adjust
themselves to new situations in a lively manner.

Mr. Hughes is baffled yet intrigued by the actions of
his family. And who wouldn't be with four children as
various in manner and actions as Jean, the studious
member of the group; Teddy, her funny and fancy-
free brother; Mildred, her sophisticated coed sister;
and Amy, the youngest, who falls in love for the first
time? Jean plays havoc with the family's plans when
she arranges a party at her home and decides to be the
life of the party. And what a party!

Those participating in the production are:

———————————————— ————————————————
———————————————— ————————————————
———————————————— ————————————————
————————————————

Life of the Party is under the direction of ———————.
The technical staff is composed of the following mem-
bers:

———————————————— ————————————————
————————————————

If you like parties as well as we do, won't you join
us ——————— evening, at the ——————— auditorium
for an evening of fun and merriment?

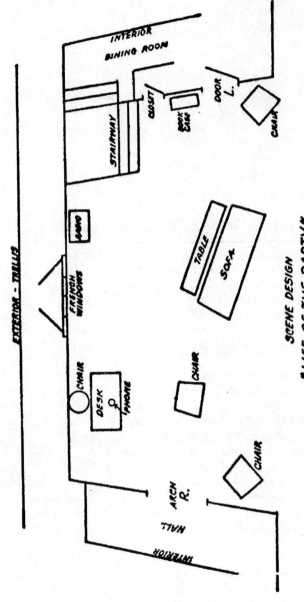

SCENE DESIGN
"LIFE OF THE PARTY"

Also By
Marrijane Hayes and Joseph Hayes

And Came the Spring

A Change of Heart

Come Over to Our House

Head in the Clouds

June Wedding

Life of the Party

Mister Peepers

Once in Every Family

Penny

Quiet Summer

Turn Back the Clock

Please visit our website **samuelfrench.com** for complete
descriptions and licensing information

SAMUEL FRENCH STAFF

Nate Collins
President

Ken Dingledine
Director of Operations,
Vice President

Bruce Lazarus
Executive Director,
General Counsel

Rita Maté
Director of Finance

ACCOUNTING

Lori Thimsen | Director of Licensing Compliance
Nehal Kumar | Senior Accounting Associate
Glenn Halcomb | Royalty Administration
Jessica Zheng | Accounts Receivable
Andy Lian | Accounts Payable
Charlie Sou | Accounting Associate
Joann Mannello | Orders Administrator

BUSINESS AFFAIRS

Caitlin Bartow | Assistant to the Executive Director

CORPORATE COMMUNICATIONS

Abbie Van Nostrand | Director of Corporate
Communications

CUSTOMER SERVICE AND LICENSING

Brad Lohrenz | Director of Licensing Development
Laura Lindson | Licensing Services Manager
Kim Rogers | Theatrical Specialist
Matthew Akers | Theatrical Specialist
Ashley Byrne | Theatrical Specialist
Jennifer Carter | Theatrical Specialist
Annette Storckman | Theatrical Specialist
Dyan Flores | Theatrical Specialist
Sarah Weber | Theatrical Specialist
Nicholas Dawson | Theatrical Specialist
David Kimple | Theatrical Specialist

EDITORIAL

Amy Rose Marsh | Literary Manager
Ben Coleman | Literary Associate

MARKETING

Ryan Pointer | Marketing Manager
Courtney Kochuba | Marketing Associate
Chris Kam | Marketing Associate

PUBLICATIONS AND PRODUCT DEVELOPMENT

Joe Ferreira | Product Development Manager
David Geer | Publications Manager
Charlyn Brea | Publications Associate
Tyler Mullen | Publications Associate
Derek P. Hassler | Musical Products Coordinator
Zachary Orts | Musical Materials Coordinator

OPERATIONS

Casey McLain | Operations Supervisor
Elizabeth Minski | Office Coordinator, Reception
Coryn Carson | Office Coordinator, Reception

SAMUEL FRENCH BOOKSHOP (LOS ANGELES)

Joyce Mehess | Bookstore Manager
Cory DeLair | Bookstore Buyer
Sonya Wallace | Bookstore Associate
Tim Coultas | Bookstore Associate
Alfred Contreras | Shipping & Receiving

LONDON OFFICE

Anne-Marie Ashman | Accounts Assistant
Felicity Barks | Rights & Contracts Associate
Steve Blacker | Bookshop Associate
David Bray | Customer Services Associate
Robert Cooke | Assistant Buyer
Stephanie Dawson | Amateur Licensing Associate
Simon Ellison | Retail Sales Manager
Robert Hamilton | Amateur Licensing Associate
Peter Langdon | Marketing Manager
Louise Mappley | Amateur Licensing Associate
James Nicolau | Despatch Associate
Martin Phillips | Librarian
Panos Panayi | Company Accountant
Zubayed Rahman | Despatch Associate
Steve Sanderson | Royalty Administration Supervisor
Douglas Schatz | Acting Executive Director
Roger Sheppard | I.T. Manager
Debbie Simmons | Licensing Sales Team Leader
Peter Smith | Amateur Licensing Associate
Garry Spratley | Customer Service Manager
David Webster | UK Operations Director
Sarah Wolf | Rights Director

GET THE NAME OF YOUR CAST AND CREW IN PRINT WITH SPECIAL EDITIONS!

Special Editions are a unique, fun way to commemorate your production and RAISE MONEY.

The Samuel French Special Edition is a customized script personalized to *your* production. Your cast and crew list, photos from your production and special thanks will all appear in a Samuel French Acting Edition alongside the original text of the play.

These Special Editions are powerful fundraising tools that can be sold in your lobby or throughout your community in advance.

These books have autograph pages that make them perfect for year book memories, or gifts for relatives unable to attend the show. Family and friends will cherish this one of a kind souvenier.

Everyone will want a copy of these beautiful, personalized scripts!

ORDER YOUR COPIES TODAY!
E-MAIL SPECIALEDITIONS@SAMUELFRENCH.COM
OR CALL US AT 1-866-598-8449!